SSR Paper 21

I0100060

Parliaments' Contributions to Security Sector Governance/ Reform and the Sustainable Development Goals:

Testing Parliaments' Resolve in Security Sector Governance During Covid-19

Wilhelm Janse van Rensburg,
Nicolette van Zyl-Gous
and Lindy Heinecken

DCAF Geneva Centre for Security Sector Governance

]u[
ubiquity press
London

Published by
Ubiquity Press Ltd.
Unit 322–323, Whitechapel Technology Centre
75 Whitechapel Road, London E1 1DU
www.ubiquitypress.com

DCAF – Geneva Centre for Security Sector Governance
Maison de la Paix, Chemin Eugène-Rigot 2E, P.O. Box 1360
CH-1211 Geneva 1, Switzerland
www.dcaf.ch

Text © Wilhelm Janse van Rensburg, Nicolette van Zyl-Gous
and Lindy Heinecken 2022

First published 2022

Cover photograph © Parliament of RSA

Print and digital versions typeset by Siliconchips Services Ltd.

ISBN (Paperback): 978-1-914481-20-8
ISBN (PDF): 978-1-914481-21-5
ISBN (EPUB): 978-1-914481-22-2
ISBN (Mobi): 978-1-914481-23-9

Series: SSR Papers
ISSN (Print): 2571-9289
ISSN (Online): 2571-9297

DOI: https://doi.org/10.5334/bcr

The full text of this book has been peer-reviewed to ensure high academic standards. For full
review policies, see https://www.ubiquitypress.com/

Suggested citation:
Janse van Rensburg, W., van Zyl-Gous, N., and Heinecken, L. 2022. *Parliaments' Contributions to
Security Sector Governance/Reform and the Sustainable Development Goals: Testing Parliaments'
Resolve in Security Sector Governance During Covid-19.* London: Ubiquity Press.
DOI: https://doi.org/10.5334/bcr. License: CC-BY-NC

To read the free, open access version of this book
online, visit https://doi.org/10.5334/bcr or scan
this QR code with your mobile device:

Table of Contents

List of Abbreviations and Acronyms

AFP	Armed Forces of the Philippines
COA	Commission on Audit
Covid-19	Coronavirus Disease of 2019
CPBRD	Congressional Policy and Budget Research Department
CSF	Covid Support Force
DCAF	DCAF – Geneva Centre for Security Sector Governance
DCC	Defeat Covid-19 Ad-Hoc Committee
DILG	Department of Interior and Local Government
DMA	Disaster Management Act
DOD	Department of Defence
ECQ	Enhanced Community Quarantine
GAA	General Appropriations Act
GOCC	Government-Owned or Controlled Corporation
ICISS	International Commission on Intervention and State Sovereignty
IPCC	Independent Police Complaints Commission
IPU	Inter-Parliamentary Union
LGU	Local Government Unit
MDG	Millennium Development Goals
MDP	Metro Police Department
MP	Member of Parliament
NAO	National Audit Office

NATO	North Atlantic Treaty Organization
NGA	National Government Agencies
NGO	Non-Governmental Organisation
NHS	National Health Service
NPCC	National Police Chiefs Council
OHCHR	Office of the United National High Commissioner for Human Rights
OSCE	Organisation for Security and Co-operation in Europe
ORCID	Open Researcher and Contributor ID
PMG	Parliamentary Monitoring Group
PNP	Philippine National Police
PPE	Personal Protective Equipment
PSIRA	Private Security Industry Regulatory Authority
R2P	Responsibility to Protect
RSA	Republic of South Africa
SABC	South African Broadcasting Corporation
SANDF	South African National Defence Force
SAPS	South African Police Service
SDG	Sustainable Development Goals
SDG16	Sustainable Development Goal 16
SIA	Security Industry Authority
SIGLA	Security Institute for Governance and Leadership in Africa
SSG	Security Sector Governance
SSR	Security Sector Reform
UN	United Nations
UNDP	United Nations Development Programme
UNOCD	United Nations Office on Drugs and Crime
UK	United Kingdom
USA	United States of America

SSR Papers

The DCAF SSR Papers provide original, innovative and provocative analysis on the challenges of security sector governance and reform. Combining theoretical insight with detailed empirically driven explorations of state-of-the-art themes, SSR Papers bridge conceptual and pragmatic concerns. Authored, edited and peer reviewed by SSR experts, the series provides a unique platform for in-depth discussion of a governance-driven reform agenda, addressing the overlapping interests of researchers, policy-makers and practitioners in the fields of development, peace and security.

DCAF, the Geneva Centre for Security Sector Governance is dedicated to improving the security of states and their people within a framework of democratic governance, the rule of law, respect for human rights, and gender equality. Since its founding in 2000, DCAF has contributed to making peace and development more sustainable by assisting partner states, and international actors supporting these states, to improve the governance of their security sector through inclusive and participatory reforms. It creates innovative knowledge products, promotes norms and good practices, provides legal and policy advice and supports capacity-building of both state and non-state security sector stakeholders.

About the Authors

Dr Wilhelm Janse van Rensburg is a Researcher at the Parliament of South Africa that specialises in parliamentary defence oversight, and a Research Fellow at the Security Institute for Governance and Leadership in Africa (SIGLA), Stellenbosch University.
ORCID: https://orcid.org/0000-0003-2659-6781

Ms Nicolette van Zyl-Gous is a Researcher at the Parliament of South Africa and specialises in parliamentary oversight of the police and policing statutory bodies.

Prof Lindy Heinecken is a Professor of Sociology in the Sociology and Social Anthropology Department, Stellenbosch University.

Competing Interests

There was no conflict of interest in producing this research report. As the research method was documentary analysis, ethical approval was not required. However, given the affiliation of the researchers to the Parliament of South Africa, institutional permission to conduct the research was obtained to ensure that there were no competing interests.

Declaration

The views expressed in this publication do not in any way reflect the opinion or views of DCAF, the Geneva Centre for Security Sector Governance.
This book has been peer reviewed by multiple experts within the subject area.

Acknowledgements

The authors would like to thank all those who provided input and feedback on the manuscript, notably Professor Mario Aguja at Mindanao State University, Nadia Dollie from the Parliament of South Africa and William McDermott, Alexandra Preperier and Merle Jasper at the DCAF. We also thank the anonymous peer reviewers for their constructive and valuable feedback on the publication. The research would also not have been possible without the institutional support from the Parliament of South Africa and the Parliamentary Research Unit.

Executive Summary

The United Nation's Sustainable Development Goal (SDG) 16 calls for the establishment of peaceful, just and inclusive societies. The security sector has the potential to contribute to SDG16 through the fulfilment of its traditional and non-traditional security tasks. However, the security sector can also detract from SDG16 when it acts outside the confines of the law. Good governance of the sector is therefore a prerequisite to achieving SDG16, and parliaments can make an important contribution to accountability and good governance. Parliaments contribute to both transparency and accountability of the sector through their various functions and act as a counterweight to executive dominance, including in the executive's use of security forces. Yet, in times of crisis, states run a risk of executive dominance and executives are often quick to resort to the use of the security sector to address an array of challenges. This risk also emerged during the global Covid-19 pandemic where states used the security sector, notably the military and police, in various ways to respond to the pandemic. This study reviewed the utilisation of the security sector in South Africa, the Philippines and the UK during the first year of the Covid-19 outbreak, resulting in varied outcomes ranging from positive humanitarian contributions to misconduct and brutality that led to the death of citizens. The initial lockdowns in these countries constrained parliamentary activity, resulting in a lack of adequate parliamentary oversight of security sector utilisation when it was most needed. Parliaments did recover oversight of the sector to varied degrees, but often with limited depth of inquiry into the Covid-19 deployments. To prevent the security sector from detracting from SDG16, the study identified a need for a rapid parliamentary reaction capability to security sector utilisation, especially in cases of extraordinary deployments coupled with an elevated risk of executive dominance.

CHAPTER 1

Introduction

The United Nation's (UN) Sustainable Development Goal (SDG) 16 calls for the establishment of peaceful, just and inclusive societies, demonstrating clear links to the security sector. However, the security sector's contribution to these outcomes are predicated on it being an accountable, effective and inclusive sector with human rights and the rule of law as points of departure (OSCE 2019: 1). The security sector therefore requires careful management to maximise its contribution to the establishment and maintenance of peaceful and just societies, demonstrating a need for effective Security Sector Governance (SSG). The ideals postulated in SDG16 of just and inclusive societies, as well as the requirement for an accountable security sector based on the rule of law, align closely with the ideals of liberal democracy such as individual rights, political pluralism, constitutionalism and the separation of powers (Heywood 1997: 26–32). This raises the question as to what contribution the institutions of democracy can play not only in SSG, but in contributing to SDG16?

This research is founded on two overarching contributions of the security sector to peaceful, just and inclusive societies. First, the security sector directly contributes to the achievement of peace, security and stability, which the UN notes as a prerequisite for sustainable development itself. This contribution requires an effective and professional security sector. Second, the security sector contributes to peace and stability through accountability. In the absence of accountability, abuse of power by the security sector undermines the attainment of peaceful and just societies. For the security sector to positively contribute to SDG16, effective systems of governance and checks and balances are required. Parliaments, as democratic institutions and pivotal actors in the separation of state powers, play a key role in governments' contribution to SDG16 through the security sector. This has particular relevance to three security sector role-players, namely the military, police and private security, that represent the direct contact points with the populace. Parliaments' impact on SSG is largely carried out through its key functions, specifically legislation, oversight, representation and budgeting. The execution of these functions form part of broader SSG, thus impacting on the security sector contribution to SDG16.

How to cite this book chapter:
Janse van Rensburg, W., van Zyl-Gous, N., and Heinecken, L. 2022. *Parliaments' Contributions to Security Sector Governance/Reform and the Sustainable Development Goals: Testing Parliaments' Resolve in Security Sector Governance During Covid-19.* Pp. 1–9. London: Ubiquity Press. DOI: https://doi.org /10.5334/bcr.a. License: CC-BY-NC

Using the two overarching contributions of the security sector to SDG16, this research explores how parliaments use their key functions to assist government, through the security sector, to achieve SDG16. This is analysed by focusing on the role the security sector has played during the global Covid-19 pandemic in selected countries. The UN noted security sector power abuses in several states, often resulting in violence that disproportionately affected marginalised groups (Namugwe 2020). Analysing the roles that parliaments played during the pandemic provides insight into their potential contribution to the maintenance of peaceful, just and inclusive societies.

Aim and research methodology

The primary aim of the study is to review the potential contribution of parliaments to SDG16 through its contribution to SSG, with the following objectives. First, to review parliaments' impact on ensuring the security sector's contribution to peace and stability (Chapter 2). Second, parliaments' contribution to security sector accountability is reviewed (Chapter 3). These contributions by parliaments to SDG16 are then practically evaluated by referring to the role of the security sector during the Covid-19 pandemic in three case studies (Chapter 4). The potential contribution of the study is reflected in recommendations to parliaments on the institutional contributions to SSG and SDG16 (Chapter 5).

In terms of methodology, a comparative case study design was adopted. This approach involves the detailed and intensive analysis of a few exemplary cases that provide suitable context for the research questions. Cross-national research is particularly valuable as it allows one to examine particular issues by comparing the different socio-cultural, political and military settings, while at the same time seeking explanations for similarities and differences to gain a deeper understanding of the phenomena studied (Bryman 2008: 54–58). In this regard, the cases selected enabled us to compare and contrast the role of the different parliaments, the methods of accountability and role of the security sectors during the Covid-19 pandemic and ultimately to establish the institutional contributions to SDG16. While an inductive approach was adopted, the aim was also to see to what extent the data supported broader theoretical arguments related to civil oversight of the security sector and enabled us to generalise by drawing on the findings from the comparable cases.

The comparative case study design was conducted in two phases. First, a theoretical foundation was established by locating SSG, the SDGs and parliaments within theory. This section relied on the analysis of existing theory and analysis, specifically on the roles of parliaments. Second, three countries were selected for a study, namely South Africa, the Philippines and the United Kingdom (UK). This selection was considered of comparative value in terms of the security sector's involvement in responding to the Covid-19 pandemic (See Chapter 4). However, the unit of analysis was the different parliaments in these countries, how they provided oversight and held the security forces accountable. The research method for the case studies was primarily documentary analysis. This was considered the most efficient way to gather data on the subject under review and insight into security sector roles during the global Covid-19 pandemic, as well as the interplay thereof with parliamentary oversight.

A wide range of documentary sources were consulted on how states, and particularly parliaments, dealt with the issue of Covid-19 in relation to the security forces. These included research articles and publications, official documents deriving from the state, mass media outputs and virtual outputs such as internet sources. Issues of authenticity, credibility, representativeness in terms of views, and evidence were guiding criteria informing document selection. In terms of official documents deriving from the state, these included Acts of Parliament and official parliamentary reports on the security forces, their deployment, conduct and mechanisms of accountability. This included parliamentary debates, questions and answers and other documentation related to the reporting on security sector utilisation during Covid-19. In addition, a heterogeneous group of additional sources were consulted, some of which are in the public domain such as annual reports, press releases and minutes of meetings. Another important source of information were mass-media releases, especially those pertaining to the use of force and abuse by the security forces in the respective countries.

In interpreting the documents and sources of information, a qualitative approach was adopted in terms of the content analysis. The aim was to establish the underlying themes to discern what issues were raised in relation to the security forces deployment during the Covid-19 pandemic, and overlay this with existing themes around SSG and parliamentary oversight, in order to do a thematic analysis. Throughout, as researchers, we were mindful of the authenticity, credibility, representativeness and meaning of the different opinions and views expressed in the documents in terms of our interpretation of the data generated from the texts.

Conceptual demarcation: SSG and the SDGs

Linking SSG and the SDGs requires defining the two concepts, as well as locating them within broader security paradigm shifts. Of particular importance in terms of global security thinking is the shift from state-centric thinking on security to the concept of human security. The post-Cold War period has been characterised by a change in the concept of national security and its specific focus on external military threats. Societal, economic and ecological threats became increasingly important in maintaining national security (Buzan 1991: 122–134). Given that these threats pose dangers to individuals, the concept of security expanded to include individual or human security. The shift in security thinking also manifested in the UN approach to development, specifically in the post-Cold War context. The 1994 UN Human Development Report highlighted human security thinking as a revolutionary shift. It noted human security's unique features as posing a universal concern, requiring early intervention, that it is people-centred and that its components are interdependent (UNDP 1994: 22–23). These features of human security thinking have specific implications for the interpretation of the SDGs and broader SSG.

The Sustainable Development Goals

The SDGs stem from the UN Millennium Development Goals (MDG), set in place in 2000, with eight specific goals aimed at alleviating extreme poverty and hunger; achieving universal primary education; promoting gender equality; reducing child mortality; improving maternal health; combatting disease; ensuring environmental sustainability; and developing global partnerships for development. At the conclusion of the MDG in 2015, the UN stated that the programme revealed the success of global action networks. The UN expressed that '[a] bold new agenda is emerging to transform the world to better meet human needs and the requirements of economic transformation, while protecting the environment, ensuring peace and realizing human rights. At the core of this agenda is sustainable development…' (United Nations 2015: 9). The 2030 Agenda for Sustainable Development was subsequently developed for implementation from 2016, aiming to build on the MDGs to eradicate extreme poverty while simultaneously focusing on economic, social and environmental facets of sustainable development. The programme set 17 SDGs that encompass the various facets of sustainable development, each with a set of targets for implementation (United Nations 2016).

In its 2015 concluding report on the MDGs, the UN found that despite successes in achieving some of the targets, progress was not universal and vulnerable societies and/or segments of societies lagged behind. Specifically, the UN noted that conflict remains a major impediment to human development (United Nations 2015: 8). The eight MDGs lacked specific focus on conflict reduction and the need for security and, as such, the Agenda for Sustainable Development addressed this requirement with the inclusion of a specific related goal. SDG16 was developed to 'promote peaceful and inclusive societies for sustainable development, provide access to justice for all and build effective, accountable and inclusive institutions at all levels'. Factors underpinning the development of SDG16 included conflict in several parts of the world, varying global homicide rates, high levels of unsentenced prisoners, the non-registration of births and human trafficking, specifically children (United Nations 2016: 40–42). These factors clearly demonstrate the broadening of the scope of security to include human security. Human security as a theme transcends the 10 targets set under SDG16:

- **16.1** Significantly reduce all forms of violence and related death rates everywhere.
- **16.2** End abuse, exploitation, trafficking and all forms of violence against and torture of children.
- **16.3** Promote the rule of law at the national and international levels and ensure equal access to justice for all.
- **16.4** By 2030, significantly reduce illicit financial and arms flows, strengthen the recovery and return of stolen assets and combat all forms of organised crime.
- **16.5** Substantially reduce corruption and bribery in all their forms.
- **16.6** Develop effective, accountable and transparent institutions at all levels.
- **16.7** Ensure responsive, inclusive, participatory and representative decision-making at all levels.
- **16.8** Broaden and strengthen the participation of developing countries in the institutions of global governance.
- **16.9** By 2030, provide legal identity for all, including birth registration.
- **16.10** Ensure public access to information and protect fundamental freedoms, in accordance with national legislation and international agreements.

In addition to the 10 targets, two 'means of implementation' targets are also included in SDG16:

- **16A** Strengthen relevant national institutions, including through international cooperation, for building capacity at all levels, in particular in developing countries, to prevent violence and combat terrorism and crime.
- **16B** Promote and enforce non-discriminatory laws and policies for sustainable development.

Viewed through the human security lens, a number of role-players are involved in SDG16 including individuals, civil society, international organisations and state institutions. This conglomerate of role-players adds to the notion that human security is people-centred rather than state-centred (Ferreira 2007: 239). However, while all these role-players contribute to human security, the function of the state is often central. The state's role in security is amplified by the fact that traditionally it has been viewed as the sole provider of security against internal and external threat and that it maintains a monopoly on the legal use of force (Born 2003: 69). The power of civil society also varies among countries, specifically between developed and developing states, as does the potential contributions of private institutions to security (Hyden et al. 2003).

To achieve the envisaged outcomes of SDG16, specific attention ought to be paid to the function of the state in ensuring human security, both from an implementation and accountability point of view. Furthermore, the contribution of other role-players to human security requires attention, including the coordination of cooperation among such role-players involved in the security sector. Effective management of the security sector is therefore essential and there is an irrevocable link between SSG and the attainment of SDG16.

Security Sector Governance

SSG as a concept consists of two components, namely the 'security sector' and 'governance'. Defining the security sector is important due to the development of human security as a concept that has broadened the parameters of the 'security sector'. Given the focus of the UN on human security, and the focus of this paper on the UN SDGs, it is of value to consider the UN's definition of the security sector. The UN Development Programme (UNDP) and Human Development Report categorise the security sector as follows (UNDP 2002: 87):

- Organisations authorised to use force including, inter alia, the armed forces, police, paramilitary forces, gendarmeries and intelligence services.
- Civil management and oversight bodies including, inter alia, presidents or prime ministers, security advisory bodies, legislatures and legislative select committees.
- Justice and law enforcement institutions including, inter alia, judiciaries, justice ministries, prisons, prosecution services, human rights commissions and ombudspersons.
- Non-statutory security forces including, inter alia, liberation armies, guerrilla armies, private security companies and political party militias.
- Non-statutory civil society groups including, inter alia, professional groups, the media, research organisations, religious organisations and non-governmental organisations (NGOs).

From the categories identified by the UNDP, the shift away from state-centred security (as reflected in the first two security sector categories) is evident and the inclusion of non-state security actors emerges. This broadening has implications for the governance of the security sector. Governments still play a key role in the governance of the security sector through, for example, policy and strategy formulation as well as funding. However, the fact that other actors influence the security realm implies that governments now perform governance of the security sector in cooperation with non-state actors. 'Considering security from the perspective of governance is useful because it includes the roles and responsibilities of government, but it also highlights how different kinds of state and non-state actors influence security provision, management and oversight in both positive and negative ways' (DCAF 2015b: 2). The multi-actor character of governance extends to various levels of governance, reflected in local, national and regional or global governance. SSG at regional or global level is largely driven through inter-governmental cooperation, along with other transnational actors (Hänggi 2003: 6).

As an expanding concept, SSG has transformed into a multi-faceted, multi-actor and multi-level endeavour. However, Hänggi (2003: 8) reminds us that '[s]ecurity sector governance combines the concepts of "security" and "governance" at the state level', thus emphasising the centrality of the state or at least a central political authority. This is premised on the reality that all aspects affecting human security are, at some level, subject to a governance system affected by formal or non-formal political authorities (Hänggi 2003: 7). The degree of influence of non-state security actors in SSG and the centrality of the state will therefore differ vastly between countries. In addition, a comparative study by Ghebali and Lambert (2004) demonstrates that SSG differs between countries and regions, largely influenced by what they term a 'democracy deficit' and limited regional integration. Despite this apparent disjuncture in the SSG architecture, there are overriding principles that enables broad-based analysis thereof. These principles are based on the concept of good governance, which UN Resolution 64/2000 includes as being 'transparent, responsible, accountable and participatory government, responsive to the needs and aspirations of the people'. These values also underscore the principles of good SSG that include accountability, transparency, the rule of law, the participation of all in decision-making, responsiveness, effectiveness and efficiency (DCAF 2015b: 3).

The correlation between good governance and the principles of good SSG further manifests in the increased focus on the democratic governance of the security sector. The focus on democratic SSG is reflected in UN literature such as the UNDP Human Development Report (2002: Chapter 4) that highlights the non-violent nature of democracies and the fact that it presents opposing groups with a myriad of conflict resolution means. The Report proposes several principles of democratic SSG, with an overarching theme for 'a demand for accountability'. Hänggi's (2003: 14) review of the norms and standards of democratic SSG developed by various international and regional bodies also emphasises 'accountability' as fundamental. Although no singular SSG oversight model exists, DCAF – Geneva Centre for Security Sector Governance (DCAF) identified key features of such oversight, including that the executive branch of government determines security policy, but remains accountable to citizens. The security services execute government security policy within the confines of the law as ensured through a constitutional judicial authority, while transgressions by security personnel or political decision-makers are dealt with through the justice system. Parliaments ensure accountability through oversight, deliberation and budgetary control and special statutory oversight bodies to oversee specific security aspects are created. Individuals, the media and civil society contribute to research and debate around security matters and reflect a variety of views and platforms for security sector accountability (DCAF 2015b: 15).

Locating the role of parliaments

Parliaments, democracy and ensuring accountability

The previous section noted the role of parliaments in SSG, but parliaments are located differently depending on varying political systems. Fuior (2011: 3–6) highlights the different structures in relations between the parliaments and the executive in presidential systems, semi-presidential systems and various forms of parliamentarism and that these relational structures impact on studies of the role of parliaments in SSG. Nonetheless, some commonality can be found in the three core functions of democratic parliaments including legislation, representation and scrutiny. In the context of modern democracies, the functions of parliaments have largely shifted to scrutiny, while the executive increasingly takes responsibility for drafting legislation (Olson et al. 2008: 201). The scrutiny function is achieved through the practice of parliamentary oversight which, in itself, is closely linked to democratic theory. Oversight is intrinsically linked to the principle of representation, which underpins parliaments as institutions. Obiyo (2006: 4) states that parliaments 'enable the People to acquire a perception of itself, of how "it" *qua* represented in the executive branch, is carrying out its Will'. Oversight can therefore be seen as a crucial component of ensuring effective rule by the people. It represents the practical means of ensuring a system of checks and balances and guaranteeing executive accountability and responsiveness.

The rise of democratic SSG and the focus on accountability arguably provides an elevated role for parliaments in SSG. This connection can largely be attributed to parliaments' democratic nature as they link to the well-established theories of democracy in two key ways. First, parliaments historically originated through the need for a consultative process in governance. Second, parliaments embody the notion of representation, with Members of Parliament (MPs) authorised to represent communities and to act on their behalf (Damgaard 2000: 3; Hague & Harrop 2007: 305). Representation ensures that the will of the people is reflected at governmental level, albeit mostly a majoritarian will (Lijphart 1999: 30). The value of these traditional views on the role of parliament in SSG is echoed by Fuior (2011: 7), stating 'parliaments provide the needed democratic legitimacy to decisions that affect people's lives. People must have confidence in the democratic system and must believe that democracy will create the conditions which will open the door to improvements in their security...' A further feature of parliaments' democratic nature can be found in the pluralist view of democracy that emphasises the stabilising role of legislatures that constantly work against authoritarianism (Alford & Friedland 1992: 71–73; Rozenberg 2018: 158–160). Stability is ensured through a balance of power founded on the separation of powers between the executive, legislature and judiciary. By ensuring that no segment of government assumes outright power, the separation of powers doctrine creates scope for accountability.

While the theoretical link between democracy and parliaments' accountability function is apparent, it raises the question as to how these institutions practically effect accountability. As indicated, parliaments play a role in legislation, even when this function has largely shifted to the executive. Parliaments remain vested with the interrogation and approval of such legislation and, as such, introduce a stage of accountability in the legislation process (although the power and willingness of parliaments in this regard varies widely between countries) (Heywood 1997: 298). Nonetheless, parliaments can still be considered effective oversight institutions given the unique set of tools they have to oversee executive action. General consensus exists among scholars on the main oversight tools available to parliaments, which commonly include committee hearings; hearings in the plenary; commissions of inquiry (including ad hoc committees); parliamentary questions; question time in the plenary; and interpellations (Izah 2013: 6; Olson et al. 2008: 10; Pelizzo et al. 2004: 4; Yamamoto 2007: 11). In addition, oversight visits or fact-finding missions to review actions on the ground serve as a potential valuable tool in parliamentary oversight (Cover & Meran 2013: 43). The utilisation of these oversight tools, or the lack thereof, provides a framework within which to analyse parliamentary oversight.

Linking parliaments, SSG and SDG16

Parliaments' three core functions can be expanded in the context of SSG. DCAF extrapolates these into five key parliamentary functions that influence SSG, namely parliaments' legislative, oversight, representative, budgetary and elective functions (DCAF 2015a). Key to discussions around SDG16 is determining how parliamentary functions apply to SSG. Parliaments' budgetary function relates to the approval, amendment or rejection of the budget for the security sector, which is essential to ensure transparency and accountability (Born 2003: 131–135). In terms of oversight, several important focus areas can be identified, specifically in relation to the security sector. First, debate around security sector legislation and policies are reflected in reviews of parliamentary oversight of the security sector (Cover & Meran 2013: 40; Yamamoto 2007: 76). Second, ensuring accountability in security sector procurement is crucial, specifically in large scale military procurement (Born 2003: sec. VII). Third, ensuring professionalism of human resources in the security sector links to democratic SSG (Born 2003: sec. VII). Fourth, the actual employment of the security sector requires oversight. The latter also relates to parliaments' legislative function, 'that determine the mandate, function, organisation and powers of security providers, management and oversight institutions' (DCAF 2015a). When parliaments have no role to play in this regard, it represents a severe limitation to security sector oversight (Born 2003: 119–120). Finally, some parliaments also play an elective role in terms of the appointment of, or scrutiny of, top security sector appointments. While the elective function represents an important facet of SSG, the direct impact on the implementation of SDG16 is likely to be limited as it relates moreover to policy approaches that are better served through the remaining four parliamentary functions.

Table 1 draws a correlation between all aspects raised in the sections above, including good governance, SSG and parliamentary functions as well as how these relate to SDG16. From the Table it is clear that several SDG16 targets have a direct correlation with the principles of good SSG. Key to note is that Parliaments' oversight function contributes to both accountability and transparency that is directly related to SDG16 which, in turn, aims to ensure public access to information (SDG16.10), develop effective accountable and transparent institutions (SDG16.6), and reduce

Table 1: Linking parliaments, SSG and SDG16.

Good governance	Good SSG	Parliamentary functions	SDG16	
			Specific SDG16 targets	Overarching SDG16 targets
Transparent governance	Transparency: Information is freely available and accessible.	Oversight function: Utilisation of parliamentary oversight tools, a high level of inquiry and the publication of information flows between parliaments and the executive.	16.10 Ensure public access to information and protect fundamental freedoms. 16.6 Develop effective, accountable and transparent institutions at all levels.	SDG16 targets effected by all functions of parliament and contributing to broader good SSG: 16.7 Ensure responsive, inclusive, participatory and representative decision-making at all levels.
Responsible governance	Rule of law: All institutions, including security institutions, are subject to the rule of law.	Legislative function: Approval of security laws, policies and international treaties. Oversight function: Oversight of policy implementation.	16.3 Promote the rule of law at the national and international levels and ensure equal access to justice for all.	16A Strengthen relevant national institutions for building capacity to prevent violence and combat terrorism and crime.
Accountable governance	Accountability: Clear expectations for the security sector with independent oversight authorities.	Oversight function: Oversight of security sector procurement, policy and personnel. Budgetary function: Ensuring accountability for the spending of parliamentary approved/allocated funds.	16.6 Develop effective, accountable and transparent institutions at all levels. 16.5 Substantially reduce corruption and bribery in all their forms.	16B Promote and enforce non-discriminatory laws and policies for sustainable development.
Participatory government	Participation: Opportunities for all to participate in decision-making.	Representation function: Public participation through popular representation and public involvement in parliamentary processes.	16.7 Ensure responsive, inclusive, participatory and representative decision-making at all levels.	
Responsive to the needs of the people	Responsiveness: State institutions that are sensitive to the varying security needs of the population. Effectiveness: Institutions fulfil their roles and responsibilities to a high professional standard. Efficiency: Institutions make the best use of their resources.	Oversight function: Oversight of security sector employment. Budgetary function: Ensuring that budgets enable the security sector to fulfil their functions and monitoring the spending of funds to ensure efficiency of the sector.	16.1 Reduce all forms of violence and related death rates everywhere. 16.6 Develop effective, accountable and transparent institutions at all levels. 16.2 End all forms of violence and torture against children.	

corruption and bribery (SDG16.5). Parliaments' legislative function is aligned to the promotion of the rule of law (SDG16.3) and inclusive, participatory decision-making (SDG16.7). The budgetary functions of parliaments further align with security-specific SDG outcomes as the appropriate funding of the security sector has the potential to contribute to reduce all forms of violence (SDG16.1 and SDG16.2). An argument can be made that the remainder of the SDG16 targets are indirectly influenced by efficient SSG. The link between parliamentary functions and effective SSG reveals that parliaments can play a direct role in the achievement of SDG16 through their legislative, representation, budgetary and oversight functions. If executed well, parliamentary oversight therefore not only contributes to an effective and efficient security sector (which directly contributes to achieving human security), but contributes to a transparent and accountable security sector. This contribution is ultimately a key determinant in the achievement of peaceful, just and inclusive societies as per SDG16.

Conclusion

SSG rests on two anchor concepts, namely effectiveness and accountability. Both these concepts permeate SDG16 and its set of targets, highlighting the important role of the security sector in its achievement. Parliaments play a key role in ensuring both security sector effectiveness and accountability through the utilisation of their legislative function, the application of their oversight tools on security sector-specific focus areas, ensuring public participation through their representation function, and fostering fiscal accountability through their budgetary function. The following chapter focuses on parliaments' role in ensuring security sector effectiveness and the direct contribution this has on SDG16.

CHAPTER 2

Parliaments and SSG—Contributing to Stability for Sustainable Development

Introduction

One of the main features of good SSG relates to 'effective and efficient security institutions'. Given the established interplay between good SSG and the envisaged outcomes of SDG16, it follows that an effective and efficient security sector is required to optimise its contribution to SDG16. But does the expanding concept of security, to include human security, impact the security sector's potential to contribute towards SSG? This chapter reviews the potential areas in which the security sector is able to contribute towards SDG16, both in terms of its traditional roles and in terms of the expanded definition of human security. In addition, the role of parliament vis-à-vis the contributions of the security sector to SDG16 is reviewed. Born (2003: 19) states that 'there is a widespread belief that security policy is a "natural" task for the executive as they have the necessary knowledge and can act quickly [and that] parliament tends to be regarded as a less suitable institution for dealing with security issues'. This chapter therefore explores opportunities for parliaments to aid the security sector in its contributions to SDG16.

Military contributions to SDG16

Samuel Huntington (1957: 11), one of the most noteworthy contributors to theory on democratic civil-military relations, states that a professional military practices the unique task of the 'management of violence'. This view aligns strongly with the historic 'war-making' nature of states and the aligned combat-centred role of the military. However, Huntington's theory focusing on the professional military has come under increasing scrutiny, including through the emergence of the concept of human security that challenges the core traditional focus of the military on

How to cite this book chapter:
Janse van Rensburg, W., van Zyl-Gous, N., and Heinecken, L. 2022. *Parliaments' Contributions to Security Sector Governance/Reform and the Sustainable Development Goals: Testing Parliaments' Resolve in Security Sector Governance During Covid-19.* Pp. 11–21. London: Ubiquity Press. DOI: https://doi.org /10.5334/bcr.b. License: CC-BY-NC

the management of violence. Hudson and Henk (2013: 7) therefore raise the question whether the roles of the military can be expanded to include non-traditional roles to meet the requirements of the expanded concept of security? Given the focus of SDG16 on the establishment of just, peaceful and inclusive societies, the potential contribution of the military to SDG16 in both its traditional and non-traditional roles requires review.

The traditional 'war-making' role of militaries does not naturally align with the developing security focus on human security. However, given the UN observation that global conflict remains a major impediment to human development, conventional military capacity is often required to address the threats such conflicts pose to human security. One of the primary functions of militaries is the protection of the state's independence, territorial integrity and sovereignty (Born 2003: 53). To achieve this end, conventional military capabilities are required to address both inter- and intra-state conflict. Inter-state conflict has decreased significantly since the Cold War, giving rise to military restructuring and defensive military postures. For example, the Organisation for Security and Co-operation in Europe (OSCE) Code of Conduct on Politico-Military Aspects of Security appeals to participating states to only maintain militaries commensurate with individual or collective security needs (OSCE: 1994). Nonetheless, some states' independence and sovereignty still face the threat of inter-state conflict and, despite the reduction in inter-state conflict after the Cold War, global inter-state tensions maintain the risk of conventional inter-state conflict. The prevalence of such tension and its bearing on the military is reflected in, for example, the 2018 USA National Defense Strategy that states 'We are facing increased global disorder, characterized by decline in the long-standing rules-based international order—creating a security environment more complex and volatile than any we have experienced in recent memory. Inter-state strategic competition, not terrorism, is now the primary concern...' (US Department of Defense 2018: 1) The traditional, conventional role of the military in maintaining security can therefore not be discarded despite the addition of non-traditional military roles.

While inter-state conflict decreased in the post-Cold War period, the prevalence of intra-state conflict emerged as a significant threat to state sovereignty. The lack of an appropriate conventional military capability has the potential to create a security vacuum which can be exploited. This is of specific relevance in states with a plethora of social, political and economic developmental concerns which are more susceptible to intra-state conflict (Ghebali & Lambert 2004: 71). The 2020 emergence of an insurgency in Mozambique's Cabo Delgado Province, the inability of the Mozambican military forces to counter the insurgency, and the resultant humanitarian impact provides a recent example of the interplay between military capacity, socio-economic concerns and intra-state conflict (Fabricius 2020). The threat of both inter- and intra-state conflict clearly allows scope for the responsible defensive use of military power in its traditional role to contribute to security and stability. The utilisation of the military in this capacity aligns with SDG16.1 that aims to reduce all forms of violence and related death rates, as well as SDG16A that calls for the strengthening of national institutions to prevent violence.

Global inter- and intra-state conflicts have also affected the non-traditional roles of the military in the pursuit of peace. The post-Cold War period saw the rise of the significance of international military interventions, including international peacekeeping and peace enforcement operations (Dandeker 2013: 40). Born (2003: 54–55) notes that militaries are used to contribute to international peace first to prevent conflict and the spill over effects of such conflict and, second, to contribute to human security by protecting civilians in conflict areas. The latter focus was formalised by the UN at its 2005 World Summit where member states committed to the principle of the Responsibility to Protect (R2P) (United Nations 2005). R2P focuses on the responsibility of states to prevent internal conflicts and other man-made catastrophes, react to situations of serious humanitarian crises and rebuild, particularly after a military intervention (ICISS 2001: Chapter 3). While Scheffer (2008) correctly notes that not all atrocity crimes necessarily justify military intervention, conventional military capacity arguably remains an important tool for the international community to react to conflict, as is reflected in the high number of UN- and regionally-backed peacekeeping operations. Peace enforcement requires even more focus on conventional military capacity to ensure the reaction capability required under R2P. Former UN Secretary-General, Dag Hammarskjöld, summarised this need by stating that 'peacekeeping is not a soldier's job, but only a soldier can do it' (Stam 2019). Through its role in R2P and international peacekeeping and peace enforcement, the military contributes to SDG16.1 (reducing violence and deaths) and SDG16.2 (end abuse, exploitation and trafficking). In the case of SDG16.2, military intervention can contribute to the international rule of law and reduce violence against women and children that are particularly affected in armed conflict (United Nations 2008).

While peacekeeping roles may be a non-traditional role of the military, it is akin to its traditional conventional role. However, the majority of security outcomes envisioned under the expanded definition of security fall outside traditional military roles (Hudson & Henk 2013: 7). As such, the military finds itself increasingly faced with the requirement for non-traditional tasks as states seek to address human security needs. These functions typically include 'humanitarian and disaster relief, the rebuilding of infrastructure, counter-terrorism, provision of public order, monitoring of election results, as well as various kinds of … peacekeeping' (Dandeker 2013: 41). These non-traditional tasks have been met with scepticism by some scholars that note these functions as irrelevant to the military and leading to the imposing of military solutions to non-military problems. Despite academic scepticism, globally the rise of non-traditional requirements on the military continues, adding to the need for military leadership to be able to do more than simply managing violence (Hudson & Henk 2013: 11–12). Where used responsibly, military utilisation in its non-traditional role can add value to several SDG16 targets. Through support to disaster relief, the military can reduce unnecessary deaths (SDG16.1) while cooperation with law enforcement agencies can promote the rule of law (SDG16.3), combat organised crime (SDG16.4 and SDG16A) and combat terrorism (SDG16A).

While the utilisation of the military can contribute towards several SDG16 targets, it does not come without challenges and the military itself can also detract from SDG16 through the abuse of its powers. Two key requirements therefore emerge for militaries to effectively contribute to SDG16. First, a capable military is required for its impact to be significant and, second, accountability for the use of the military is required to ensure its utilisation does not detract from SDG16. While the latter will be addressed in Chapter 3 of this study, the following section reviews how parliaments can contribute to an effective and capable military to ensure its optimal contribution to SDG16.

Parliaments' role in enhancing military contributions to SDG16

National defence and security and the functioning of the military is considered a national competency in most countries as reflected in, for example, Article 4(2) of the European Union's Lisbon Treaty. The oversight function of defence will therefore sit with national parliaments, rather than sub-national parliaments. The powers of national parliaments in relation to national defence varies across political systems, depending largely on constitutional directives on its powers (Fuior 2011: 3). Nonetheless, the legislative, budgetary, representation and oversight roles of parliament noted in Chapter 1, as well as the focus areas for oversight of the security sector, continue to find application across parliaments. Given the potential contributions of the military to SDG16, it then raises the question as to how the national parliament can utilise its roles to enhance the contribution of the military to SDG16?

Parliaments' legislative function is important in ensuring a legislative regime within which military contributions to SDG16 can be realised. Legislation that ensures the responsible utilisation (deployment) of the military is key, including the purposes for and conditions of deployment. Through legislation, parliaments can ensure that human security needs are reflected in conditions of military deployment. Legislation ought to outline principles for both domestic and international military deployments and parliaments can ensure that legislation is aligned with the outcomes envisaged in SDG16. For example, domestic military deployments in cooperation with other state departments during humanitarian crises can be used to address human security. However, legislation needs to ensure that humanitarian assistance remains the ultimate goal of such deployments. Esterhuyse and Heinecken (2015: 79) highlight the potential pitfalls of 'domestic deployments [as it can] have an undermining influence on military professionalism, more specifically by severing the relationship with certain parts of the population or the political elite'. Legislation is therefore not only required to balance the need for addressing human security, but also for the maintenance of civil-military relations.

In terms of international deployments, legislation should stipulate under which conditions external deployments are permitted. In order for deployments to aid in achieving human security, the principles of R2P should reflect in deployment legislation. The 128th Inter-Parliamentary Union (IPU) Assembly Resolution called 'on parliaments to take all the necessary measures to bring their countries' criminal and military law into line with international norms on the protection of civilians in armed conflict...' (IPU 2013). Most importantly, parliaments can ensure that domestic legislation on external military deployment aligns with international treaties, specifically the UN Charter of which Article 2.4 requires states to refrain from the external use of force that is inconsistent with the purposes of the UN (United Nations 1945). In the case of non-UN multilateral and bilateral treaties or agreements, parliaments have the responsibility to ensure that these align with SDG16's aim to promote just, peaceful and inclusive societies, specifically where joint military deployments outside the UN framework are considered. Crucially, public involvement in the ratification of treaties, through parliament, should be encouraged (Born 2003: 34). This adds another layer of assurance that treaties, and any potential military deployments, are aligned with human security needs and will therefore align with SDG16.7 (ensuring responsive, inclusive, participatory and representative decision-making).

In addition to the appropriate legislative framework, parliamentary oversight of deployments ensures the optimal contribution of militaries to SDG16. Parliamentary oversight of deployments can be performed both *ex ante* and *ex post*, with practices varying between states (Pelizzo et al. 2006: 13). In states with *ex ante* parliamentary oversight of deployments, the impact on SDG16 targets could form part of debates around the decision to deploy the military. In turn, in states where parliaments have only *ex post* oversight, the alignment of the deployment with SDG16 targets could impact on parliamentary decisions to terminate such deployments. Of specific value are questions around SDG16.1 (whether a deployment reduces violence), SDG16.2 (whether a deployment reduces violence against children), SDG16.3 (whether a deployment contributes to the rule of law), SDG16.4 (whether a deployment aids in the reduction of illicit arms flows) and SDG16A (whether a deployment prevents violence and combats terrorism and crime). The parliamentary oversight tools noted in Chapter 1 provide the practical means for conducting deployment oversight. Questions by MPs as well as House debates around deployments, when appropriately publicised, are important contributors towards broader societal debate on the utilisation of the military (Born 2003: 42). Through these tools, MPs have the means to question the executive on the contribution of deployments to specific SDG16 targets and disseminate deployment information to the public. The parliamentary committee system in particular can be used to track deployment contribution to SDG16 targets, including through a special inquiry if needed.

To maximise deployment contributions to specific SDG16 targets, efficient and fit-for-purpose military forces are required. The 'power of the purse' (budgetary) function of parliaments is important in this regard as it allows parliaments to continuously monitor expenditure (Born 2003: Chapter 23). Unforeseen military deployments are not always budgeted for and may require additional funding. The approval of such funds and subsequent oversight of expenditure, as well as a legal framework to ensure oversight of ad hoc operational funds, are crucial to ensure mission effectiveness. For example, Esterhuyse and Heinecken (2015: 79) find that 'professionalism of African militaries is regularly undermined by corruption through wasting of defence money on irrelevant equipment and military personnel focusing their attention on private financial endeavours'. This observation applies not only to African militaries but has global application and highlights the negative impact of a lack of oversight of deployment expenditure on military capacity. Transparency International further found, in a 2013 study on the quality of parliamentary oversight of the military, that only 33% of the 82 countries surveyed publish detailed and transparent defence budgets. Parliaments' budgetary function includes the requirement for a range of reports and reviews throughout the budget execution phase, which invariably include military deployments (Cover & Meran 2013: 32). It is therefore essential that MPs are familiar with the main aims of a deployment, how these align with specific SDG16 targets, and whether expenditure is appropriate to practically achieve such targets.

Parliaments' budgetary function is also important in periods preceding deployments, specifically in terms of military education and training. Sufficient funding should be made available to ensure that training achieves the required output, as this aligns with SDG16.6 (accountable and transparent institutions) as well as SDG16A (strengthening relevant national institutions). Military training itself should be structured to ensure that militaries are familiarised with human security needs and how these relate to SDG16. This is reflected in, for example, the OSCE (1994: 4) Code of Conduct on Politico-Military Aspects of Security that states: 'participating States will make widely available in their respective countries the international humanitarian law of war. They reflect, in accordance with national practice, their commitments in this field in their military training programmes and regulations'. Parliamentary activities can ensure that budgets and policy directives on training align with mission outcomes that contribute to the establishment of just and peaceful societies.

Finally, parliamentary oversight should also take into account the multi-dimensional nature of non-traditional deployments. Government departments do not generally function in isolation and for military deployments, specifically domestic deployments, to contribute to just and peaceful societies, effective cooperation is required. Janse van Rensburg (2019: 78) identifies oversight of interdepartmental cooperation involving the military as a key lower-order focus area for parliamentary defence committees. Committees are ideally located to conduct oversight of the levels of cooperation between government departments, and they can do so in conjunction with other portfolio committees. Where cooperative deployments take place between, for example, the military and police forces, parliamentary oversight should ensure that the mission outcomes are practically aligned with SDG16.

Police contributions to SDG16

SDG16's ideals for just and inclusive societies, as well as the requirement for an accountable security sector based on the rule of law, align closely with the ideals of liberal democracy. It is therefore imperative that the function of policing align with these democratic principles in order to contribute effectively to SDG16. Internationally agreed principles guide democratic and effective policing as key aspects of good SSG. Although there is no consensus on the definition of democratic policing, 'progress thereto necessitates a shift from a control-orientated approach to a more service-orientated approach that is responsive to the needs of the public and focussed on proactive crime prevention' (OSCE 2008). The agreed characteristics of democratic policing include upholding the rule of law; human rights and police ethics; accountability and transparency; and a public service orientated policing approach (DCAF 2019). A responsive policing approach, cognisant of public need and based on the aforementioned characteristics, aligns with the shift towards human security.

The rule of law is arguably the most important feature of democratic governance and thus democratic policing, which is crucial for the achievement of the 2030 Agenda and the SDGs (DCAF 2020). There is a strong link between peaceful societies and sustainable development, as the UN states, 'The rule of law is fundamental to international peace and security and political stability; to achieve economic and social progress and development; and to protect people's rights and fundamental freedoms' (United Nations, n.d.). In simple terms, the rule of law means that no one is above the law, which makes the role of the police to discharge their duties within the confines of domestic legislations, international instruments and human rights norms and standards vitally important to build not only police legitimacy, but also state legitimacy. The rule of law is an intrinsic link to the protection of the individual's fundamental rights and freedoms which, in turn, is a key function of the police and lies at the heart of democratic policing. The rule of law further lies at the core of SDG16's focus on establishing 'just' societies.

Given the centrality of the rule of law to SDG16, the functions of police services as entities that maintain the rule of law permeate all aspects of SDG16. The police are the entry point of the criminal justice system value chain and has significant impact on the entire security sector's capacity to improve human security (UNODC 2011). If police arrest and detain individuals on an arbitrary basis, outside the confines of the law, it collapses the entire chain and detracts from the SDGs as a collective (DCAF 2020). As such, democratic policing is characterised by certain minimum functions that the police must perform, within the confines of the law. Key policing functions include the prevention and detection of crime; the maintenance of public order; the protection of the individual's fundamental rights and freedoms; the reduction of fear; and rendering assistance to the public (UNODC 2011). These functions underpin various targets set under SDG16, such as reducing all forms of violence and related death rates (SDG16.1); ensuring equal access to justice for all (SDG16.3); protecting children from abuse, exploitation, trafficking and violence (SDG16.2); significantly reducing illicit financial and arms flows (SDG16.4); substantially reducing corruption and bribery in all their forms (SDG16.5); developing effective, accountable and transparent institutions (SDG16.6); ensuring public access to information and protect fundamental freedoms, in accordance with national legislation (SDG16.10); as well as the promotion and enforcement of non-discriminatory laws (SDG16B). To achieve these targets, well-resourced and trained police, in terms of both capital and human resources, are crucial. Proactive police operations must uphold the principles of democratic policing and the police must execute targeted crime prevention operations fairly.

In most states, the police represent the main state security provider and 'the most visible manifestation of government authority performing the most obvious, immediate and intrusive tasks to ensure the well-being of individuals and communities' (OSCE 2008). In practical terms, the police play a significant role in achieving SDG16 through simply being effective, professional and adhering to democratic policing principles. However, the police also have the potential to detract from achieving SDG16 as they are vested with significant powers to suspend individual freedoms, notably the power to use force, to arrest and to detain. Chapter 3 of this study addresses the aspects of accountability through civilian control, notably parliaments, and measures to prevent the misuse of policing powers. Yet, parliaments, through the accountability process, play an important role in contributing to effective and professional democratic policing.

Parliaments' role in enhancing police contributions to SDG16

Unlike military institutions which are generally overseen by national parliaments, oversight of policing is impacted by the state structure and type of political system. Federal states, for example, may consist of police services that are decentralised and function with a higher level of autonomy compared to centralised states. In federal states, the oversight role of national parliaments may therefore be limited. Similarly, presidential systems may provide less scope for parliamentary oversight than parliamentary systems, depending on the level of executive control that the president has over the police (Aguja and Born 2017: 11–17). Despite these restrictions, national parliaments maintain an important oversight function which, in most countries, would even extend to federal police services. In Belgium, MPs may submit questions on the functioning of the local and federal police, while in India 'the Home Minister is responsible for all police functions and accountable for their actions to Parliament and, at the state level, to the Assembly' (Aguja and Born 2017: 18, 101–102, 18). The latter also demonstrates the value of sub-national parliaments in oversight of police services. For example, while not a federal state, the provincial parliaments in South Africa (along with the national parliament) conduct oversight of provincial-specific policing issues, as well as municipal police services in the country's larger metropolitan areas (White Paper on Policing (South Africa) 2016).

While some limitations apply to the role of national parliaments in police oversight, this does not negate the role such institutions play in terms of police services and such oversight efforts could be read in conjunction with the oversight roles of sub-national parliaments. Through their ongoing reviews of police activity, parliaments not only contribute to police accountability (See Chapter 3), but they play a role in enhancing police contributions to SDG16 through reviewing police actions at various stages of implementation. In *ex ante* oversight of police actions, parliaments set the direction for the police through its legislative function. Police legislation must be well drafted, clear and easy to understand by both the public and police officer (DCAF 2020). This clarity is crucial to contain (and limit) the police's coercive power to suspend individual rights and freedoms. The main legislative contribution by parliament to enhance the police's contribution to SDG16 is to ensure that governing legislation aligns with democratic policing principles, codes of conduct and human rights standards as codified through various regional and international instruments. This alignment will give effect to SDG16.6 seeking to develop effective, accountable and transparent institutions at all levels. Constitutions generally codify these human rights that must find a strong footing in all legislation pertaining to the police (OSCE 2008). According to the OSCE (2008), police legislation should define:

- The functions of the police.
- The people that constitute the police.
- The requirements for working as a police officer.
- The powers that the police have to carry out their functions.
- When and how the police can use their powers.
- How the use of police powers is to be reported.

It usually also specifies:

- How police are financed.
- The authority to which the police are to report.
- The overall authority.

As noted, the police have the potential to detract from achieving SDG16, specifically when they act outside the parameters of the legislation. A key countermeasure to abuses of power are independent police oversight bodies that investigate police misconduct and criminality, thereby strengthening the rule of law (Bruce 2017). It is crucial that parliaments establish these oversight bodies in law and, similar to the governing legislation for policing, parliaments must dictate their functions and investigative powers. These bodies must account to parliaments rather than to the executive branch of the government (Amnesty International 2015). The existence of such bodies not only adds to police accountability, but contributes specifically to SDG16.5 and SDG16.6.

In addition to parliaments' *ex ante* oversight role through legislation, *ex post* oversight of the actual functioning of policing is crucial. Parliaments can contribute to effective and efficient democratic policing through executing its budgetary function that includes amending, adopting and monitoring police budgets. Herein lies a significant parliamentary power to scrutinise proposed policing budgets that could highlight possible over/underfunding for the police as a whole, or specific divisions. The budgetary allocation of the various policing divisions should also align with human security needs. For example, a disproportionate allocation to police services for the protection of dignitaries, at the expense of rendering services to the public, detracts from many outcomes envisaged under SDG16. Adequate funding for police operations and training is crucial to effect policing contributions to SDG16 targets. An underfunded police service cannot be effective or efficient in reducing violent crime and foster security and stability that is conducive to development (Kavanagh, Wardell and Park 2020). Similar parliamentary budgeting impacts on policing oversight bodies as they can only execute their functions through adequate resourcing, while remaining accountable to parliament.

Key to parliaments' *ex post* oversight of the functioning of the police is parliamentary committees. Ordinarily, parliaments have dedicated and permanent committees mandated to oversee the police (UNODC 2020). These include the power to summon members of the executive and senior police management, conduct site inspections, initiate parliamentary investigations and invite independent experts. It is important that parliaments do not exclusively rely on the police for information but also use the tools available to them, notably thematic experts and site inspections (UNODC 2011). The UNODC states that 'these parliamentary instruments are crucial tools to monitor whether police act in the framework of laws, strategies and policies developed and adopted by the legislative and the executive' (UNODC 2020). In addition, parliamentary committees scrutinise strategic planning documents and annual reports as part of ongoing oversight. These are crucial documents to identify measurable targets, as well as oversight of the achievement of targets such as the reduction of violent crime, crimes against women and children and corruption. Parliaments can further play a role in preventing the police from detracting from SDG16 targets through utilising its oversight tools. For example, parliaments can consider the establishment of ad hoc committees to conduct oversight of specific actions that detract from SDG16, such as procurement corruption (SDG16.5) or abuses of policing powers (SDG16.6) (UNODC 2020).

Private security contributions to SDG16

Chapter 1 noted the UNDP's categorisation of the security sector into five distinct areas that include all sectors that contribute to activities that uphold the general social order, including state and non-state actors, or statutory and non-statutory actors. These include, for example, social or religious organisations, armed groups and private security companies. This study makes specific reference to the private security industry's role in terms of policing and excludes reference to, for example, private military companies. The exclusion is primarily based on the limitations that parliaments often have in terms of oversight of private military companies and the varying degree of legislation guiding private military companies globally (Bailes & Holmqvist 2007: 10–12). The specific focus on the private security industry's role in terms of policing further aligns with the case studies to be presented in Chapter 4. Private military companies undoubtedly have the potential to both contribute to or detract from SDG16 and the impact of parliaments on directing or influencing this contribution may present a subject for further academic inquiry outside the scope of this study.

DCAF (2015b) states that 'in many countries actors engaged in non-state policing are more numerous, better trained, better resourced and more powerful than the state police or law enforcement agencies'. As such, these actors play an important role in the security sector and have the potential to contribute to SDG16. Through maintaining security, the private security industry can reduce violence (SDG16.1), reduce violence against children (SDG16.2), promote the rule of law (SDG16.3), combat organised crime (SDG16.4) and promote and enforce non-discriminatory laws (SDG16B). The contributions to SDG16 is of specific relevance to the private security industry's role in relation to policing. However, the private security industry can also detract from SDG16, notably through the demotion of inclusive societies and increasing unequal access to security and justice.

A main concern with the proliferation of private security is that it widens the inequality gap between rich and poor, especially when the rich can 'by-pass the state' to buy safety, a basic human right (Provost 2017). The fundamental distinction between private security and the public police is in the client base. The private security industry serves paying clients as opposed to the public police that ought to serve all citizens equally, thereby implying that 'citizens will get the level of protection they can pay for' (Sparrow 2014). According to *The Guardian*, At least half the world's population lives in countries where there are more private security workers than public police officers' and that more than 40 countries have more private security providers than police officers (Provost 2017). For example, China has an estimated 5 million private security providers compared to 2.7 million police officers. (Provost 2017).

The core policing mandate of public police has grown and changed considerably over time, especially in the 21st-century. Increasingly, public police are drawn into areas beyond their traditional roles (visible policing and crime investigation). Given these expanded roles, it may be unrealistic for the public police to be everywhere all the time. The private security sector can fulfil the role of a force multiplier based on its geographic footprint and sheer numbers. However, there is pushback from both the public police and the private security sector, largely based on accountability and distrust. The increasing encroachment of the private security sector into public spaces, which is the traditional mandate and legislative space of public police, further compounds the pushback (Montgomery & Griffiths 2015).

Private security can play a meaningful role in crime prevention, and thus SDG16, through either outsourcing of police functions or collaborative partnerships with police. Many international jurisdictions focus on outsourcing a portion of traditional policing services, such as foot patrols, forensic services and intelligence gathering. Other countries, such as the UK and the United States of America (USA), utilise both approaches. In the UK, significant cuts to the police budget drove outsourcing and an increasing threat of terrorism drove collaboration. An example of a successful public-private-partnership between private security and police is Project Griffin, launched in the UK as a counter-terrorism initiative after the 2001 terrorist attacks on the World Trade Centre in New York. This partnership is considered best practice and was implemented in various countries, including Singapore, Australia, Canada and the USA. The USA also uses both outsourcing and collaborative partnerships, with outsourcing of certain security functions playing a significant role. It is estimated, for example, that '70% of the budget for U.S. intelligence agencies is provided via subcontracts to private corporations' (Montgomery & Griffiths 2015).

The key challenges to a collaborative approach and outsourced policing duties relate to accountability, transparency and the principles of democratic policing (Montgomery & Griffiths 2015). The public police are subjected to a strict legal and regulatory framework as opposed to the private security sector that only reports to its employers. In most countries, there is no formalised policy framework to guide outsourcing or collaboration, nor is there a public oversight body to ensure accountability, especially in relation to human rights abuses (Montgomery & Griffiths 2015). In the UK, attempts have been made to extend the powers of the then Independent Police Complaints Commission (IPCC)[1] to oversee the functions and operations of private security guards that perform policing duties, but these have not been successful.

Parliaments' role in enhancing private security contributions to SDG16

Given that private security falls largely outside the scope of governance by the executive, parliamentary powers in terms of such service providers remain comparatively limited (Bryden and Caparini 2006). This further implies that where opportunity for parliamentary oversight exists, it will fall within the ambit of the national parliament rather than sub-national parliaments. The question remains whether parliaments can play a role in maximising the contribution of police outsourcing or collaborative policing to the mentioned SDG16 targets. In lieu of existing best practice, parliaments can give careful consideration to the increased focus on private security and crime prevention cooperation. These partnerships need a formalised approach with strong guidelines based on a clear policy and legal framework. This must include regulatory requirements, strategic and operational management and it ought to be subject to civilian oversight (Bryden & Caparini 2006). Alignment with democratic policing principles must be maintained and potential scope for broader parliamentary oversight of such collaborative approaches be explored.

Much like parliaments' role in enhancing police contributions to SDG16, parliaments play a role in the private security sector's contributions thereto, specifically in terms of legislation and regulation. According to the UN, regulation should extend to as many of the wide-ranging activities of the private security sector to avoid loopholes, ensure accountability and maximise the contribution of private security to crime prevention and community safety (UNODC 2014). Legislation can be used to create a regulatory system, which is aligned to SDG16.6 (developing accountable and transparent institutions), and should include:

- Authorisation and limitations of services.
- Appropriate licensing systems.
- Code of professional conduct.
- Use of weapons, force and detention.
- Safety and working conditions of security service providers.
- Training standards.
- Complaints mechanism.
- Independent investigative bodies, such as an Ombud.
- Oversight and accountability mechanisms.
- Sanctions for infringements.

Regulatory authorities should monitor the adherence by private security providers to legislative prescripts through compliance inspections and, in turn, these authorities should be accountable to parliaments. Ordinarily, parliamentary committees dedicated to oversee the police are mandated to oversee the regulation of private security as part of its contribution to peace and security. Parliaments can summons these regulatory authorities, conduct site inspections, initiate parliamentary investigations and invite independent experts. Although parliaments will not ordinarily conduct site inspections at private companies or summon the owners of privately owned companies, this is not beyond the remit of parliaments. In addition, parliamentary committees scrutinise strategic

---

[1] The Independent Police Complaints Commission was re-established as the Independent Office for Police Conduct in 2017 through the Policing and Crime Act, 2017.

planning documents and annual reports of regulatory authorities as part of ongoing oversight. Parliaments can further play a role in preventing the private security sector from detracting from SDG16 targets through utilising its oversight tools. For example, parliaments can consider the establishment of ad hoc committees to conduct oversight of specific actions that detract from SDG16, such as abuses of policing powers (SDG16.6) (UNODC 2020).

Conclusion

This chapter focused on the contribution of the security sector to achieving sustainable development by reviewing the utilisation of the military, police and private security. It highlighted that the security sector has the potential to contribute practically to the outcomes of SDG16. The military is uniquely placed to react to domestic and international threats to human security, while the police is the main state law enforcement agency and directly charged with crime prevention and upholding social order. Through collaborative approaches, the private security sector can also be drawn in as a contributor to SDG16 outcomes. Through its legislative and oversight functions, parliaments can enhance the contribution of the security sector to SDG16 by ensuring effective, sufficiently funded and appropriately trained security forces cognisant of the requirements of sustainable development. However, while the security sector has the potential to contribute to sustainable development, this contribution should be subject to an important caveat in that it should not be misused to validate securitisation. 'Security and justice are essential for peace and development, but they should be defined in terms of how people across society experience them: the primary goal is human security...' (Möller-Loswick 2017). Parliaments, as counterweight to executive dominance in democratic systems of checks and balances, are essential instruments in ensuring that the security sector is not misused and detracts from human security. Effective oversight of and legislating for all role-players in the security sector ensures transparency and accountability, which is essential for contributing to peaceful and just societies. The next chapter will focus on the contribution of parliaments to peace and stability through advancing transparency and accountability in the security sector.

CHAPTER 3

Parliaments and Security Sector Governance— Contributing to Just and Peaceful Societies

Introduction

Chapter 2 highlighted the positive practical contributions that the security sector can make towards achieving various targets of SDG16. It further demonstrated how parliaments use their various functions to maximise the security sector contributions. However, the utilisation of the security sector as enablers of SDG16 requires a careful balance as the sector wields significant power, given its legal authority to use force. The abuse of power by the security sector can severely undermine the attainment of peaceful and just societies. In a democratic context, it is therefore essential to ensure that sufficient checks and balances are in place to guarantee a transparent and accountable security sector as a means of preventing abuses of power.

Given the established link between democracy and parliaments' accountability function, parliaments have the potential to make a strong contribution to ensuring security sector accountability and transparency. Parliaments may well not be the panacea in addressing issues related to security sector accountability or the effective civil control of the sector, but they represent an important component of broader efforts at democratic and effective control of the security forces. The UNDP (2017: 16) recognises this potential contribution of parliaments by noting that to achieve SDG16.6 (developing effective, accountable and transparent institutions), 'parliaments will need to explore different ways of improving their work processes and systems'. This chapter focuses specifically on parliaments' contributions to SDG16.6, with emphasis on the establishment and maintenance of an accountable and transparent security sector, as well as the parliamentary processes and systems best suited to contribute to this outcome. References are also made to other SDG16 targets affected by parliaments' contributions to security sector accountability and transparency.

How to cite this book chapter:
Janse van Rensburg, W., van Zyl-Gous, N., and Heinecken, L. 2022. *Parliaments' Contributions to Security Sector Governance/Reform and the Sustainable Development Goals: Testing Parliaments' Resolve in Security Sector Governance During Covid-19.* Pp. 23–34. London: Ubiquity Press. DOI: https://doi.org /10.5334/bcr.c. License: CC-BY-NC

Security sector transparency

The post-Cold War period has been underpinned by the shift from state security to human security, which aligns with global democratisation. The Cold War period's focus on state security encompassed a significant focus on secrecy, especially around the security forces. This is evident in information on the activities of security forces that have emerged through, for example, truth and reconciliation commissions and other post-1990 investigations in a number of countries, ranging from Chile and Argentina to South Africa, Russia and the USA (Roberts 2007: 309–311). The post-Cold War period's democratic characteristics offered opportunities to enhance openness around the security forces, given the links between liberal democratic values and transparency. However, security sector transparency remains problematic worldwide. While secrecy is necessary in some instances, specifically around national security, it must be acknowledged that these claims are frequently exaggerated and over-used. Roberts (2007: 311–313) notes that the post-Cold War period did not result in any significant increases in government transparency in countries like China, Russia and Indonesia and while others became more transparent, legislation often continued to provide a veil of secrecy around information on the security sector. The terrorist attacks on the USA in September 2001 again contributed to renewed securitisation and secrecy around the sector (Tagarev 2010a: 274).

Despite setbacks in some countries in relation to transparency, ongoing post-2001 research suggests a continued 'uptake' of security sector transparency, most notably in democracies. For example, increased international information-sharing as a component of building international security points to broader embracing of security sector transparency. Yordonova (2015: 6) points to the adoption of a Resolution by the Parliamentary Assembly of the Council of Europe on the Abuse of State Secrecy and National Security (Obstacles to Parliamentary and Judicial Scrutiny of Human Rights Violations) as an example of global efforts towards transparency and scrutiny. Yordonova therefore argues that the notion of transparency as a component of national and international security has gained more widespread acceptance. This point aligns with earlier writing by Roberts (2007: 320–325) who argues that transparency can actually promote and preserve security in several ways. First, it can aid in the development of better security policy, given that access to information will allow greater societal understanding of and input into policy development. Second, transparency is an effective way of facilitating information flows within the security services themselves. This is crucial to assist officials in the security services to fulfil their functions as they themselves access information about the sector from outside the bureaucratic structures. Third, transparency prevents inertia within the security sector by allowing indirect monitoring thereof by external role-players, facilitated through the availability of official information. Security sector transparency further creates public consensus around the sector (Fluri & Lunn 2010: 58). The latter relates specifically to transparency around security sector expenditure and the requirement for openness around the utilisation of public funds.

To achieve the advantages associated with transparency in the security sector and to effectively contribute to SDG16.6, certain basic preconditions should be met. The legislative process that constitutes the security sector, its management and functioning should be open to the public. A legal framework should exist that allows an informed citizenry with the right to legally challenge and/or express its views on the security sector. Further, transparency links to accountability and therefore legal and other means should exist for the citizenry to hold its leaders accountable for security sector management. Finally, maximum public participation in security sector policy decisions, and the potential consequences of such decisions, should be fostered (Bucur-marcu 2009: 25–26). These conditions are required to ensure the public buys into security sector management and they align with the creation of a system of checks and balances that guide democracies.

For an involved citizenry, the availability of information around the security sector is paramount. The requirement for information availability is also reflected in SDG16.10 (ensuring public access to information), aiming to ensure public access to information and the protection of fundamental freedoms. Official information flow on key security sector aspects is important, with budgetary transparency of primary importance. For example, a 2011 study by Transparency International on the transparency of defence budgets in 93 countries found that only 14% of countries reflected a high level of transparency, while 65% reflect moderate to low level budgetary transparency (Gorbanova and Wawro 2011: 5). Budgetary transparency also extends to the need for transparency of security sector procurement. Elevated levels of secrecy in the security environment have resulted in it being prone to widespread corruption, particularly in newly independent states where trust in the military is low and secrecy is used as a guise for corrupt activities (Tagarev 2010b: Chapter 1). Transparency of security sector policies reflect another key area that is required to create clarity and credibility. Furthermore, the general management of the various segments of the security sector in a democratic setting requires transparency. This includes openness on aspects such as the composition and management of human resources, a clear gender perspective of the sector, the utilisation of the sector by the state and transparency around conditions such as infrastructure and morale in the sector (Born 2003).

While the areas of transparency identified above represent important points of departure in a democratic society, the actual manifestation of such transparency also requires clarity. For effective security sector transparency, official documentation must be available for public scrutiny. While this differs among countries, such documentation typically includes annual reports, budgetary reports, the publication of White Papers and other policy discussion documents, departmental strategic and annual performance plans, procurement policies, details of procurement transactions, and information produced by government entities that ensure accountability such as Ombuds institutions and parliaments. However, central to true transparency is the need for information on the security sector to be relevant, accessible, timely and accurate (Born 2003).

How do parliaments ensure security sector transparency?

Hollyer, Rosendorff and Vreeland (2011) set out to test the levels of transparency among various political systems. The authors concluded that democracies are more transparent than other regime types in terms of the availability of policy-relevant data. Parliaments, as institutions of democracy, are therefore intrinsically linked to the principle of transparency and in so doing constitute an important role-player in achieving SDG16.6 and SDG16.10. Parliament's functions, including legislating, budgeting, representation and oversight, are linked to the value chain of transparency. The process of legislating is linked to transparency through the well-established representation function of parliaments for two reasons. First, parliaments provide platforms for the debate around proposed legislation, with the process often involving opportunity for public comment. Second, the physical constitution of parliaments suggest that the citizenry has a direct say in how laws are made, through its elected representatives (Heywood 1997: 297). Representation thus provides for interplay between parliament and the citizenry, while an open legislative process fosters transparency in the rule of law. Similarly, the debate that parliaments foster opportunities for the citizenry to input into parliamentary activities also reflect in the budgetary function of the institution. Where such processes are open and transparent, it contributes to elevated levels of budgetary transparency, including in the security sector. While these parliamentary functions are key to security sector transparency, the oversight function of parliament ensures continuous transparency.

Parliaments' oversight functions are important for transparency, and while several mechanisms for oversight exist, the prominence of parliamentary committees requires specific focus. Committees are often referred to as the 'engine rooms' of parliaments, as they represent the key drivers of oversight of the executive branch of government (Calland 1997: 55). Practically, a significant proportion of a parliamentary programme's time is normally spent on committee oversight activities and, as such, the flow of information from committee activities are important to transparency. DCAF (2006) notes, however, that the achievement of transparency in parliamentary committees that oversee the security sector is inhibited by several aspects. Security sector oversight is complex and encompasses oversight of a number of departments and entities. The security sector is traditionally characterised by secrecy and there is often strong involvement of the executive. Transparency International raised similar concerns following an evaluation of the quality of legislative oversight of the military in 82 countries, concluding that poor transparency in oversight of the military is a global concern. The study revealed that while parliamentary oversight of the military is common practice, it has become increasingly 'illusionary' (Cover & Meran 2013: 3). For parliaments to contribute effectively to security sector transparency through the oversight process, the practical tools used for oversight requires optimal utilisation. In addition, the public use of these tools will enhance transparency. Chapter 1 already referred to the various tools available for security sector oversight at parliament, while Chapter 2 showed how these can be used to enhance SSG, but how do these add to transparency and SDG16.6?

Parliamentary *debates* on the security sector offer arguably the greatest opportunity for enhancing transparency, on condition that they take place publicly. Debates take place both in plenary sessions, but consistent debates on the security sector will likely be found in the various committees with an oversight mandate of the sector. They are usually characterised by a presentation from officials, policy statements, or other planning initiatives from the executive (Born 2003: 77; Yamamoto 2007: 62). They also allow MPs opportunities to robustly engage the executive and, in so doing, extract additional information that aids transparency. Despite the value of parliamentary debates being increasingly questioned in modern parliaments, Rozenberg (2018: 148) argues that debates remain valuable 'to frame ideologically a debate and therefore to link policy proposal to electoral politics' and that they bring credibility to the view of parliaments as representative institutions. Parliamentary *questions* offer a similar opportunity for MPs to extract information on the security sector. Questions from MPs to the executive are submitted orally or in written form and their importance lies in the opportunity they afford individual members to raise concerns around the security sector and garner timely responses. Parliamentary questions are generally publicly available and, where sufficient cooperation from the executive is forthcoming, contribute to the public availability of security sector information (Born 2003: 79).

Special inquiries refer to in-depth parliamentary investigations of specifically identified matters in a portfolio. These are largely conducted at committee level or can be conducted by ad hoc committees or through the establishment of subcommittees. During special inquiries, committees often request external specialists' input and may subpoena certain role-players. (Born 2003: 80; Yamamoto 2007: 39–42). Special security sector inquiries can aid transparency through the publishing of publicly accessible formal reports, as well as through the inclusion of external input at parliamentary level. Another oversight tool that contributes to transparency is *oversight or site visits* by committees to security sector facilities and deployment areas. These visits familiarise MPs with security matters at ground-level (Cover & Meran 2013: 43). Transparency follows through the publishing of official findings and recommendations that flow from observations during the oversight visit.

A final parliamentary oversight tool that adds depth to parliamentary transparency is the *use of external audit* capabilities. Transparency International notes that parliaments can assist in lowering corruption risks by including external audit analysis in their oversight (Cover & Meran 2013: 10).

Through the utilisation of external audits, parliaments can contribute directly to SDG16.5 aiming to reduce corruption and bribery. Practically, this involves parliaments, or committees, calling external auditors (or state auditors) to conduct in-depth audits of specific departmental projects and report their findings. Alternatively, state auditing institutions may conduct audits on their own volition and submit reports to parliament. These reports, when debated publicly and/or included in parliamentary findings, provide a high level of transparency. Given the noted risks of corruption in the security sector, independent audits provide an important tool to aid transparency. The contribution to transparency will, however, depend on parliaments' willingness to request and utilise external audit capacity and to publicly review the findings.

The primary tools available to parliaments to oversee the security sector adds significantly to transparency of the sector. However, as noted, the security sector is shrouded in secrecy and this often plays out at parliamentary level. To contribute to SDG16.6, parliaments, as institutions, need to be transparent about their engagements with the security sector. In practice, some important steps are required to foster this transparency. First, a culture of transparency within parliaments is required that links to the representation function of the institution. All parliamentary information is the property of the citizenry and effort should be made to engage citizens in parliamentary affairs. In terms of the security sector, this requires, for example, limited closed meetings by oversight committees and open engagement with interested parties, notably the media. Second, parliamentary information transparency should be underpinned by policies that ensure the timely publication of information and openness about the activities of the institution. Third, parliaments need to provide easy access to information that is not discriminatory in any way. Fourth, given the general accessibility of the communication channel, parliaments should enhance the electronic communication of information. This requires an open, well-structured and simple to use online platform for the citizenry to access information about the security sector (OpeningParliament.org 2012).

The overview above highlighted the difficulty in promoting transparency in a sector that is historically characterised by secrecy and demonstrated the crucial roles that parliaments can play in promoting security sector transparency through the utilisation of oversight tools and the publishing of information. While such efforts all contribute to SDG16.6 and SDG16.10 in particular, parliamentary transparency is but a means to achieve accountability as an end. True parliamentary transparency ensures both vertical accountability (holding MPs to account) and horizontal accountability (ensuring that MPs hold the executive to account) (Mills 2017). To ensure the true realisation of SDG16.6's focus on accountability, both parliamentary and security sector transparency are prerequisites.

Security sector accountability

Accountability is a key requirement for good governance and, in terms of SSG, accountability means the establishment of clear expectations for the security sector and independent oversight authorities. Accountability of the security sector aligns directly to SDG16.6, seeking effective, accountable and transparent institutions, and indirectly to SDG16.7 aiming to ensure responsive decision-making. To achieve such accountability, alignment with the democratic requirement for a balance of powers, which implies a counterweight to the power of the security sector, is required. The question around security sector accountability therefore reverts to the frequently quoted maxim of Juvenal: '*quis custodiet ipsos custodes?*' (Who guards the guardians?).

In a democratic setting, the response to Juvenal's question revolves around the concept of civil control of the security sector. This question is at the heart of theorising on civil-military relations and applies equally to the question around political control and accountability of police services. Heywood (1997: 375) notes that political control of the security services can either have positive characteristics such as accountability, scrutiny and oversight, or negative implications such as the politicisation of the sector and its utilisation to serve a political elite.[2] Samuel Huntington (1957: 83–84) proposed two ways to strike a balance between military and civilian role-players in a state. Objective control of the military focusing on the professionalisation of the military diminishes the likelihood of military involvement in state control (through coups, for example). Subjective control, on the other hand, aims to change the military structures to those similar to the state, which almost assumes military involvement in politics. Simply put, subjective control infers the disappearance of the distinction between the armed forces and government. Huntington's view has, however, been criticised for not being universally applicable or western-centric. Rebecca Schiff (1995: 12), for example, postulates that civil-military relations can be better explained by reviewing levels of 'dialogue, accommodation and shared values or objective among the military, the political elites, and society'. Rather than a separation of military and civilian powers, Schiff's 'Concordance Theory' focuses on cooperation among the various role-players.

These notable theories are important to security sector accountability as it demonstrates the need for establishing civilian control over the security sector to limit the involvement of the sector in the management of the state. More recent theories highlight that security sector accountability should not only be seen in terms of the sector's potential involvement in the management of the state, but as a constantly evolving process subject to evolving challenges. Beliakova (2021), for example, argues that civilian control of the military in democracies can erode over time through actions such as insubordination, deference of security-related policy-making to the security sector and competition between security sector and government. Of specific value is Beliakova's focus on the potential damage to civil-military relations when civilian policy-making decreases and the military's power in politics increase. Lima *et al* (2020) note a similar concern around deference of security sector policy-making in their hypothesis on 'national security neglect'. The theory proposes that "a lack of attention in national security policy-making by civilian elites can weaken political controls over the armed forces, inhibit effective defence reforms that challenge military prerogatives, and, over time, reinforce militarization in national security policymaking, especially in its three main pillars: defence, intelligence, and public safety" (Lima et al. 2020: 1). Brooks (2020: 43–44) notes the mounting pressure on militaries' non-partisan nature and calls for the development of an improved framework for military personnel's political engagement. Recent theoretical developments reveal that the maintenance of the system of checks and balances requires civilian decision-makers to be actively involved in maintaining civilian control of the security sector and not defer responsibilities to the sector itself. It further shows the need for ongoing dialogue, as noted by Schiff, and the constant re-evaluation of such dialogue, as noted by Brooks, to ensure healthy levels of civil control of the military. The role that constant dialogue and re-evaluation has in civil control of the security sector has implications for parliaments as they represent one of the institutions responsible for fostering dialogue and re-evaluation through oversight. The question then arises as to how dialogue and re-evaluation plays out practically in a democratic setting to ensure effective civil control of the security sector.

Hänggi (2003: 16) identifies five 'best practices' for the democratic control of the security sector. First, a constitutional and legal framework is required that allows for the separation of powers and a clear security sector role definition. Second, democratic control implies civilian control of the security sector. Third, parliamentary control and oversight of the sector is required. Fourth, the sector must remain subject to a sound judicial system. Fifth, public control of the sector should be encouraged through, for example, an independent media, think tanks and other academic institutions. These principles align with the 2002 UNDP Human Development Report's principles for good SSG and therefore demonstrates how the democratisation of SSG revolves around the

---

[2] Heywood's reference relates specifically to political control of the police, but applies equally to other segments of the security sector.

prominence of accountability as a requirement. But what does an effective and accountable security sector look like within a democratic context? Toornstra (2013: 13) highlights accountable security sector characteristics as follows, aligned with the UN Secretary-General's report on SSG:

- An accountable security sector is guided by a legal framework that directs the legitimate use of force within the scope of internationally accepted human rights.
- An accountable security sector is characterised by systems of governance and oversight, notably budgetary control systems and institutions to protect human rights.
- A well-structured and resourced security sector in terms of structures, personnel and equipment aids accountability.
- Transparent interoperability among various security sector role-players.
- Accountability is enhanced in a security sector that promotes unity, integrity, discipline, impartiality and respect for human rights.

The characteristics of an accountable security sector hinges on two pillars of accountability. First, a security sector that itself behaves in an accountable manner. The stated traits of an accountable security sector such as 'integrity, discipline, impartiality' all form part of the requirement for a security sector that ascribes to 'ethical conduct'. In practical terms, during security sector operations, ethical conduct relates to the understanding by the sector that it constantly remains accountable, not only to governance structures, but to local communities and, in the case of the military, even to non-combatants (Hudson & Henk 2013: 18). On a macro-level, it requires acceptance of accountability by the sector to all three branches of government. Second, an accountable security sector is highly dependent on the democratic systems of governance and oversight that ensures accountability (Born 2003: 22). The executive ensures accountability through the management of the security sector within the confines of the law and by executing control of the sector's budget and policy directives in a transparent manner. The judiciary contributes to accountability by prosecuting legal contraventions by members of the security sector. Parliaments not only pass legislation that ensures an accountable sector, but also ensures continued accountability through its oversight functions.

In addition, several other state institutions contribute to accountability. Ombuds institutions have the capacity to launch in-depth investigations into alleged wrongdoings by members of the security sector. This is of particular importance in ensuring security sector accountability to communities as Ombuds institutions primarily investigate complaints by the public and therefore serve as a mechanism to build public trust in the sector (Born 2003: Chapter 16). A well-capacitated government audit institution ensures financial accountability of the security sector. It further adds to the sector's accountability to communities by ensuring that taxpayers get value for money in terms of security sector expenditure (Born 2003: Chapter 24). An internal audit capacity within the various security sector departments adds a layer of accountability in terms of corporate governance. Internal audit has been shown to serve as a predictor for accountability and serves as an important tool in terms of risk management (Tumwebaze et al. 2018). Accountability can further be ensured through the creation of legislative institutions that have investigative and other legal powers over the security sector departments. Examples include Public Protector Offices, Human Rights Commissions and other legally established investigative commissions.

Security sector accountability is crucial in a democratic context and, through the development of systems of checks and balances, numerous institutions of accountability have developed over the years. However, for accountability to manifest, civil authorities capable of exercising political control and enforcing such accountability are essential (Ghebali & Lambert 2004: 35). In this sense, parliaments play an important role as they serve not only as institutions that ensure accountability, but also as conduits to ensure the optimal functioning of all state institutions contributing to accountability.

Parliamentary focus areas to ensure security sector accountability

Griffith (2005: 4–5) highlights the view of accountability as a relational concept asking four key questions, namely who is accountable?; for what is it accountable?; to who is it accountable; and, how is accountability enforced? In terms of SSG, parliaments are key to the accountability questions posed by Griffith as the security sector is accountable to it as an institution, it possesses the tools to ensure accountability and it is backed by the legislation to enforce accountability. The remaining question is: What is the security sector accountable for? To identify these accountability indicators for the security sector, it is important to turn to the focus areas of parliamentary oversight, as well as the parliamentary budgetary function. Chapter 1 already noted several focus areas for parliamentary oversight, while Chapter 2 clarified how oversight and budgeting can contribute to effective security services that practically contribute to SDG16 targets. It was further noted how transparency around some of these focus areas is essential for good SSG and adds to the achievement of SDG16.6 and SDG16.10. However, these focus areas need to be explored further in relation to their contributions to accountability of the security sector via parliaments.

Parliaments' budgetary function and oversight of related performance aspects

One of the primary tasks of parliaments relates to the power of the purse function. Parliaments' budgetary function is a continuous process that requires *ex ante* engagement during parliaments' annual approval of national budgets, as well as *ex post* engagement of how the security sector spent its funds. Countries with robust parliamentary budgetary functions are characterised by strong committee systems where well-resourced, independent committees continuously monitor expenditure. Such monitoring includes inquiries into internal and external audits of security sector expenditure and input into future expenditure. The importance of monitoring security sector budgets is captured in indicator SDG16.6.1 that measures 'primary government expenditures as a proportion of original approved budget, by sector' (United Nations 2016). Transparency International (Cover & Meran 2013: 28–29) found in a study of 82 legislatures that, specifically in relation to defence, only 30 countries reflect a low risk in terms of budgetary oversight and debate. This demonstrates the ongoing need for development of thorough mechanisms of security sector budget monitoring. The continuous monitoring of the budget also clarifies parliaments' responsibility to review in-year expenditure as well as ad hoc audits or external reviews of security sector expenditure. This requires the executive to set clear, achievable targets for the security sector against which performance can be measured. Through these measures, parliaments ensure value for money to taxpayers as well as adherence to governments' broader strategic planning. There are, however, several factors that may inhibit effective parliamentary oversight of security sector budgeting and expenditure. A lack of transparency and limited information, often due to 'secrecy', limits parliaments' interrogative capacity. Limited information further negatively affects the ability of civil society and the media to scrutinise the budget and add to oversight through parliaments. Internal parliamentary arrangements such as limited time spent or poor parliamentary support can also detract from efficient budgeting (Born 2003: Chapter 23). A lack of transparency and parliamentary engagement impacts directly on parliaments' ability to contribute to SDG16.6 and SDG16.10.

While in-year expenditure reviews increase accountability, it can be argued that this should be expanded to include oversight of in-year performance against set targets. As noted, transparency of the security sector budget requires not only expenditure projections, but also viewing these against set targets. Two sets of security sector documents are required for parliament to fulfil this role effectively. First, annual reports of security sector activity and achievements allows for retrospective reviews of performance against set targets. A 2004 study on the importance of oversight confirms that although the actual value of annual reports varies among recipients thereof, it has become an increasingly valuable tool in ensuring accountability and, at the least, a significant source of information (Mack & Ryan 2004). Second, in-year performance documents such as quarterly reports assist in ensuring continuous accountability as they measure quarterly expenditure against quarterly targets. These documents give practical effect to public access to information of the security sector espoused to in SDG16.10.

Oversight of security sector procurement presents a budget-related focus area for oversight, notably due to the risk of corruption often associated with procurement processes in the security sector. It therefore represents an important oversight area that aids parliaments in contributing to SDG16.5 seeking to reduce corruption and bribery. Parliaments must ensure general accountability in the procurement process given its power of the purse function. More specific to its SSG function, however, is the need for the prevention of corruption as it reduces the effectiveness of the security sector, as well as public trust in the sector (Gorbanova & Wawro 2011: 3). Parliaments' role in procurement oversight is amplified by the fact that security sector procurement is often characterised by secrecy. Parliamentary committees generally have the option of calling for closed meetings or establishing ad hoc committees or subcommittees to oversee secretive procurement (Cover & Meran 2013: 52). Parliaments should also ensure the regular auditing of security sector procurement and audit information must be shared with the institution. The complexity of procurement itself and the fact that lengthy procurement processes often span over several parliamentary periods often hamstrings the oversight of security sector procurement. Institutional memory is therefore required to ensure continued oversight of procurement. Institutional memory at parliaments, in relation to procurement oversight, should be viewed in the context of SDG16A that calls for the strengthening of national institutions in order to combat and prevent crime. Toornstra (2013: 31) captures the complexity and secrecy of procurement around procurement at parliamentary level by noting that parliamentary oversight remains varied across countries ranging from limited monitoring in some states to intense scrutiny and a requirement for parliamentary approval in others.

Oversight of security sector policy

Parliaments, specifically its committee systems, offer valuable platforms for debate around security sector policy. Transparency International defines security sector policy as 'the laws, strategies, and approaches used by governments to decide on the scope and activities of the military and national security agencies' (Cover & Meran 2013: 40). Parliaments are responsible for ensuring that policy aligns with the needs of the people and is implemented accordingly, and in so doing it prevents the security sector from becoming the dominant role-player in security sector policy-making (Beliakova, 2021; Yamamoto 2007: 9). Oversight of policy therefore allows for opportunities to ensure alignment with human security needs and the SDGs.

In broader terms, parliaments play a role in setting and monitoring national security policies, which 'involves major decisions about the security sector which affect the external and internal security of state and society. It is based on a given approach to security, gives guidelines for the military doctrine, and is developed within the framework of the international and regional regulations' (Born 2003: 26). It is therefore within the ambit of national security policy that a state's orientation to and inclusion of human security would be captured. National security would dictate the security priorities, be it state security, human security or regime security. In countries that have prioritised the achievement of the SDGs, the targets of SDG16 should reflect in national security policy. Of specific value for inclusion in national security policy is the envisaged outcomes of the utilisation of the security sectors and how this can aid in achieving SDG16.

(See Chapter 2). Parliaments can add a layer of assurance to the inclusion of SDG16 targets in security policy. Through its oversight function, parliaments further ensure the actual implementation of policies aligned with the SDGs.

Oversight of security sector human resources

The aim of oversight of the security sector's human resources is to ensure that employees of the security sector remain loyal to the state and act within the confines of existing legislation, which lessens the risk of coups and other improper political involvement. Oversight of human resources further ensures fair treatment of security sector personnel and stability within the personnel contingent of the sector. On a more practical level, and specifically in relation to SDG16A (strengthen relevant national institutions), parliamentary oversight should ensure that certain aspects of professionalism are entrenched in security sector personnel. This relates to the responsibility of parliament to include training and education as a focus area for oversight to ensure accountability. Aspects to be included in training of the sector include, inter alia, the following (Born 2003: Chapter 25):

- Ensuring the allegiance of the security sector to the state, constitution and state institutions. Oversight should include determining whether the oath of office (or code of conduct) of security sector personnel take these allegiances into account. This should be aligned to the guidelines provided in the 1979 Code for Law Enforcement Officials as adopted by the UN.
- A sound internal order in the security sector. Oversight should ensure adherence to international legal frameworks and precedents. Crucially, oversight should also ensure that security sector practices make it obligatory for personnel to disobey obviously illegal commands.
- Oversight should ensure that security sector training is politically neutral, cognisant of human rights and in line with international humanitarian law.

An additional oversight focus area related to human resources relates to the need for oversight of security sector morale. Bucur-marcu (2009: 99) highlights, in term of the essentials of building defence institutions, the importance of the 'development of realistic measures of performance and maintaining a high level of morale of the entire personnel'. Oversight of morale is essential as it can detract from the positive roles that security forces can play in a state or internationally, such as their contribution strengthening national institutions. In addition, oversight of morale is essential to accountability due to the underlying reasons for a breakdown in morale. A study on SSR in Zimbabwe notes several examples of factors negatively affecting morale in the police, such as the systemic abuse of recruits, police procedural shortcuts, repressive legislation and the lack of due process, corruption, conflict between personnel and poor conditions of service (Chitiyo 2009: 14–15). Oversight of morale can therefore extract these underlying impediments to accountability. The practical oversight of morale is, however, complex and difficult to measure. Parliaments should therefore develop means to objectively assess morale be it internally or through external institutions. In this regard, DCAF notes that the offices of the inspector-general and Ombuds institutions can assist in tracking morale of the security sector (Fluri & Lunn 2010: 58).

Gender and racial equality represents another aspect of human resources in need of parliamentary oversight. Rebecca Schiff's 'Concordance Theory' of civil-military relations places a requirement on military and political leadership as well as citizens to agree on the social composition of the officer corps. This notion can arguably be expanded beyond the military to all institutions within the security sector. It is therefore unsurprising that in its 2007 study on parliamentary oversight, the World Bank identified a clear need for parliaments to focus on gender equality and mainstreaming (Yamamoto 2007: 22–23). This focus increased in recent years through, for example, the publication of the DCAF series on 'Gender and SSR: Examples from the ground' (DCAF 2011) and the OSCE Gender and Security Toolkit for Defence (OSCE 2020). Aspects of racial equity in the security sector also forms part of the desire to reach agreement on the social composition of the security sector. In fact, many countries consider it a democratic imperative that their security forces are broadly representative of the populace with respect to race, ethnic composition, social class, religion and gender. For example, the negative impact of ethnic bias in Kenya's police recruitment has been documented and can be viewed against the positive correlation between community safety perceptions and ethnically representative security forces in Kosovo (Gitari 2019; Gray & Strasheim 2016). In this regard, there are a number of reasons why diversity management has assumed greater prominence in recent years and has become subject to parliamentary oversight.

The first stems from the emphasis placed on individual rights, which have obliged the security forces to review policies and practices that discriminate against individuals, based on race, religion, gender, sexual orientation and so forth. A second reason, is to preserve their legitimacy. The general assumption being that the control of the armed forces is more or less guaranteed where all segments of society are represented. A third reason, is the growing problem of recruitment and retention in some countries, which has obliged armed forces to recruit from non-traditional pools to meet their manpower requirements. A fourth, is that diversity improves the effectiveness of armed forces, especially in terms of humanitarian missions and in terms of civil-military cooperation. There is growing evidence that a better gender/racial mix is more suited to missions linked to the R2P. In this regard, United Nations Security Council Resolution 1325 affirmed the important role of women in both the prevention and resolution of conflicts and called for gender mainstreaming to be incorporated in all multinational peacekeeping operations, not as something that is beneficial, but essential. A fifth reason is where a country needed to integrate armed forces from different ethnic, ideological and political backgrounds. This has meant that managing diversity is more than just accommodating diverse groups, but dealing with underlying tensions of cultural and ideological differences (Heinecken 2009). There is thus a clear need for considering gender and race not only in the management of the security sector, but also in the utilisation thereof. This focus will also foster further support for the SDGs, specifically indicator SDG5C: 'Adopt and strengthen sound policies and enforceable legislation for the promotion of gender equality and the empowerment of all women and girls at all levels' (United Nations 2016).

Oversight of security sector utilisation

The utilisation of the security sector arguably presents one of the most important oversight focus areas for parliaments in its quest to ensure accountability. Chapter 2 noted that the powers of parliaments vary in terms of *ex ante* and *ex post* oversight of deployments of the military, resulting in varying oversight powers among states. However, whether parliaments have approval or withdrawal rights of military deployments does not diminish the general oversight responsibility during deployments. Born (2003: 120–121) notes at least four ways in which parliaments can continue oversight of military deployments. They can request or force the executive to report to parliament on the rationale for a specific deployment. Parliaments can use their budgetary powers to impact on the deployment of the military. Parliaments can further raise continuous debate around the deployment and utilise other oversight tools such as questions and visits to ensure an elevated level of accountability. Parliaments may conduct a post-deployment inquiry to add a level of scrutiny and accountability. Parliaments may also utilise their legislative role to ensure adequate legislation around the domestic deployment of the military. Legislation should provide for clear guidelines as to when and how the military may be used domestically, as such deployments often impact negatively on military professionalism and can create division between society and the military (Esterhuyse & Heinecken 2015: 79). Continuous oversight during domestic deployments is also essential to ensure accountability of the military and to limit offences.

Police utilisation differs from the military in that they are continuously 'deployed' domestically. Continuous utilisation requires continuous oversight of the various functions for which the police are utilised. This requires an efficient parliamentary police committee characterised by a high work rate and ensuring oversight of other policing accountability institutions such as Ombuds institutions and independent police investigative institutions. Oversight should ensure accountability in cases of interdepartmental cooperation, be it between the military and police or between police and private security. Some states are increasingly seeking an integrated approach to security that goes beyond the military (Aldis & Drent 2008: 36). In such cases, parliaments are well situated to ensure accountability through their committee systems. This requires a flexible parliamentary system that can adjust easily to intercommittee cooperation.

Conclusion

The security sector is often characterised by both a lack of transparency and accountability. Yet, given the nature of its functions, it requires elevated levels of transparency and accountability. Parliaments, through their oversight functions, combine transparency and accountability as they represent the desired natural outflows of oversight. Parliaments are ideally situated to ensure transparency through the utilisation of a unique set of oversight tools. They further add to accountability of the security sector through oversight of specific focus areas relevant to the sector. Parliaments therefore contribute directly to SDG16.6 in that they aid the development of an accountable executive. By promoting transparency, they also contribute to SDG16.10 that aims to ensure public access to information, which is particularly relevant to the security sector that is often shrouded in secrecy. Oversight of security sector procurement has a further positive impact on the achievement of SDG16.5 (reducing corruption and bribery) given that such procurement is often susceptible to corruption. However, SDG16.6 stipulates the need for accountability and transparency *at all levels*, thus highlighting a requirement for an accountable and transparent parliament itself. In order for parliaments to contribute effectively to the achievement of SDG16, they must enhance accountability of the security sector and ensure their own transparency and accountability. Both these elements come under significant strain during times of extraordinary pressure on the security sector. To contextualise this, the next chapter reviews parliamentary oversight of the security sector in selected countries during the 2020/21 Covid-19 pandemic and how this relates to the achievement of SDG16.

CHAPTER 4

Covid-19 and the Security Sector Response— Testing Parliaments' Resolve and Sustainable Development Contribution

Introduction

The Covid-19 pandemic created a unique challenge that required an extraordinary response from both the executive and parliament in most states. In many states, the executive immediately resorted to utilise the security sector, notably the police and military, in its Covid-19 response through the use of emergency powers codified in their respective constitutions. This created a dichotomy in terms of states' ongoing efforts to achieve SDG16 targets. The extraordinary utilisation of the security sector could potentially either contribute positively to efforts to curb the pandemic and therefore improve human security, or it could lead to an abuse of power that detracts from the achievement of SDG16 targets. As noted in previous chapters, parliaments play an important role in managing this dichotomy as they can serve as enablers of security sector contributions to SDG16. The Covid-19 pandemic therefore offered a unique test case for parliaments' management of the potential contribution of the security sector to SDG16 through their primary tasks of legislation, representation and oversight.

This chapter reviews parliaments' approach and contribution to SSG during the Covid-19 pandemic in three countries, namely South Africa, the Philippines and the UK, and concludes with parliaments' resolve to manage security sector contributions to SDG16 targets. The case study was concluded in early 2021 and therefore only reflects on the first 12 months of state response to the pandemic in these countries. In the three cases studies, parliaments' functions came under intense pressure and, due to the impact of the pandemic, detailed scrutiny of legislation was often not practically possible. Parliaments also needed to develop innovative means to facilitate hybrid parliamentary sittings to continue their oversight mandate due to lockdown

How to cite this book chapter:
Janse van Rensburg, W., van Zyl-Gous, N., and Heinecken, L. 2022. *Parliaments' Contributions to Security Sector Governance/Reform and the Sustainable Development Goals: Testing Parliaments' Resolve in Security Sector Governance During Covid-19.* Pp. 35–60. London: Ubiquity Press. DOI: https://doi.org /10.5334/bcr.d. License: CC-BY-NC

regulations which limited in-person meetings. This created a vacuum resulting in parliaments having to 'catch up' with their core functions, notably that of holding the executive accountable for the application of legislation related to the use of the security sector. This requirement became especially pronounced where armed forces were given additional powers and responsibilities that fell outside their normal duties. Analysing the roles parliaments played during the pandemic provides insight into their potential contribution to the maintenance of peaceful, just and inclusive societies.

In line with the methodological approach adopted for the study, the selection of the case studies was informed by the need to test diverse cases of parliamentary oversight of the security sector against a common challenge, namely Covid-19, in an effort to discern whether commonalities can be extracted and lessons learnt. Security forces were used in different capacities around the world and the three case studies reflect this diversity. The case studies also reflect diverse outcomes in the utilisation of the security sector, ranging from discomfort and uncertainty around the role of the security forces in the UK to the abuse of power in South Africa and the Philippines. The countries studied have varying backgrounds regarding the utilisation of the security sector and the potential for power abuses. The UK does not have a recent history of large scale domestic military deployments and widespread power abuses by the security sector. South Africa, in turn, has a past and recent history of power abuses by the security forces against the local population during the pre-1994 *apartheid* era, yet finds itself in a new democratic era with a security agenda oriented towards human security. The Philippines has an even more recent history of militarisation with significant concerns around power abuses and human rights violations in the country (see, for example, the UN Human Rights Council Resolution 41/2 of 2020). Covid-19 presented a common threat and in all three cases the security sector was utilised in response to the threat. The three countries have parliaments in place to ensure security sector legislation as well as oversight of the sector. While South Africa and the UK function as parliamentary democracies, the inclusion of the Philippines as a presidential system allows for the further extraction of commonalities in diverse parliamentary oversight systems.

Covid-19 and the varying utilisation of the security sector

In response to the Covid-19 pandemic, states utilised their security sector in logistical, humanitarian, health and law enforcement capacities, with varying implications. The use of the military in logistic, humanitarian and health support improved the legitimacy of militaries in some cases, especially where they could respond effectively to the health emergency. However, internal deployments in law enforcement capacities also had the opposite effect, especially pertaining to the military which is not trained for law enforcement and often resulted in human rights infringements. The section below shows the different approaches taken by South Africa, the Philippines and the UK. All three countries had their militaries deployed in logistic, humanitarian and health support capacities, but differed in their approach to law enforcement deployment. In South Africa, the military was deployed jointly with the police and soldiers had powers to arrest and detain. The Philippine armed forces supported the police and participated in activities such as roadblocks, but not in a law enforcement capacity and thus soldiers did not have policing powers. In the UK, the military was placed on standby to support the police, but only in emergencies and only to free up police officers to patrol. There was significant resistance in the UK to deploying the military to support the police.

South Africa

On 15 March 2020, President Ramaphosa declared the Covid-19 pandemic a national disaster under the Disaster Management Act, 2002 (DMA) (Act 57 of 2002) via a public television broadcast. Subsequently, on 23 March 2020, the President announced a national lockdown of 21 days (26 March 2020 to 16 April 2020). The lockdown included a strict curfew, and restricted the movement of all goods and people to confinement, except specified sectors rendering essential services. Since the initial lockdown, the South African Government adopted an adjusted risk strategy imposing various levels of restrictions (as at March 2021).

As part of the lockdown, the President authorised the joint deployment of the South African Police Service (SAPS) and the South African National Defence Force (SANDF) under Section 201(2)(a) of the South African Constitution and Section 18(1) of the Defence Act, 2002 (Act 42 of 2002) with the aim to enforce the lockdown restrictions. Initially, the President authorised the employment of 2,820 members of the SANDF for services in cooperation with the SAPS in order to maintain law and order and to support other government departments to combat the spread of Covid-19. A month later (21 April 2020), the President authorised the employment of an additional 73,180 members of the SANDF, consisting of the Regular Force, Reserve Force and Auxiliary Force, in so doing putting the entire SANDF on standby for potential deployment (Parliament RSA 2020b). Ultimately, the full contingent of 73,180 was never deployed, with an average of 8,091 members deployed over the first three months of the extended deployment (PMG 2021a). Although the presidential order put the entire defence force on standby, it should be seen as a practical decision in order to avoid having to obtain approval for adjusted force levels. In June 2020, the President authorised the continued employment of the SANDF, albeit at a reduced number of 20,000 soldiers, further reduced to 2,122 in February 2021.

The SAPS, SANDF and other law enforcement agencies conducted the following activities to ensure compliance to lockdown regulations and to limit the spread of Covid-19:

- To conduct static roadblocks at all national routes and major routes in order to monitor, control and ensure adherence to the regulations.
- To conduct vehicle check points, at provincial routes, regional routes, rail routes, main streets in order to monitor, control and ensure adherence to the regulations.
- To conduct high visibility patrols at quarantine areas, taverns, taxi ranks, beaches, shopping malls, educational institutions, entertainment centres, religious centres, etc. in order to monitor, control and ensure adherence to the regulations.
- Designated investigation capacity and case management (police only).
- Monitoring the implementation of strategies through the National Operational Command Centre.

Ahead of the deployment, President Ramaphosa addressed the SANDF as Commander-in-Chief at the Doornkop Army Base in Soweto. He urged soldiers to act within the confines of the law and stated, 'This is not a moment for skop (kick) and donner (assault). This is a moment to be supportive to our people' (SABC 2020). This statement pre-empted the significant risk of domestic deployment of soldiers in law enforcement capacities. Throughout the lockdown, the SAPS remained the main state authority to enforce the lockdown restrictions. Between March 2020 and January 2021, the SAPS arrested more than 342,000 people countrywide (Mabuza 2021).

The initial period after the announcement of the hard lockdown saw several instances of misconduct in which police and soldiers abused their powers. According to media reports, law enforcement officers allegedly killed three people for lockdown infractions during the first three days of the lockdown. Various other reports emerged of SANDF soldiers forcing persons to do strenuous physical exercise to 'teach them a lesson' (to obey the law) (Cilliers 2020; Head 2020). In January 2021, the police fired water cannons at sick and disabled persons who failed to observe social distancing in a queue for government social grants (Evans 2021). In April 2020, the UN urged states to guard against law enforcement agencies using excessive and deadly force to enforce lockdowns and curfews. The UN identified South Africa as one of several countries with a 'toxic lockdown culture' due to the use of excessive force in imposing lockdown regulations (Farge 2020).

Heavy-handed lockdown enforcement by police was especially evident in informal settlements, where law enforcement officers acted drastically against minor offences (Arnold 2020). In many of these settlements, social distancing guidelines could not be observed due to spatial layout, as many structures (houses) are less than 1.5 metres apart (Oliver 2020).

The tipping point arguably came with the torture, assault and subsequent death of Mr Collins Khosa by SANDF soldiers and members of the local municipal law enforcement department in the Alexandra township in Johannesburg, two weeks after the lockdown came into effect (10 April 2020). The attack was initially not condemned and an internal SANDF inquiry found the soldiers involved not liable for the death of Mr Khosa (Marais 2020). The case was, however, referred to the Office of the Military Ombud for investigation, who found that the soldiers involved acted improperly, irregularly and in contravention of their code of conduct (Makinana 2020). The Khosa family approached the High Court of South Africa (Gauteng Division) to seek justice. The judgment condemned the actions by the SANDF and the Metro Police Department (MPD) and made several orders against the respondents. Although the SAPS was not involved in the specific case, the Judge referred to past well-documented cases of police brutality and, as such, the police were included in the orders handed down by the Court.

In addition to the law enforcement support to the SAPS, the SANDF's Covid-19 deployment included health, humanitarian and logistic support to various other government departments' Covid-19 response objectives. This was evident in the first Covid-related SANDF deployment that involved the repatriation of South African citizens from the Wuhan Province in China in March 2020. In terms of health and humanitarian support, the SANDF assisted several provincial departments of health in various capacities, including decontamination, distribution of food parcels, health screening and Covid-19 awareness education. The Military Health Services assisted in the establishment of ICU/Hi-Care facilities and rendered administrative support in the form of data-capturing of medical records at 15 overburdened hospitals across the Gauteng Province. The SANDF further supported the general running of hospitals, notably the Charlotte Maxeke Academic Hospital in Johannesburg, with services including scanning orderlies, drivers, porters, financial and human resource administration and safety and security. Logistical support included the deployment of 180 SANDF engineers in support of the Department of Water and Sanitation to provide water purification and distribution services (PMG 2020d).

South Africa has a significant private security industry and, according to the Private Security Industry Regulatory Authority (PSIRA), there were 10,298 security businesses and 2,495,899 individual security officers registered as at 31 March 2020. Of the total number of registered security officers, 548,642 were actively employed (PSIRA 2020). Due to this enormous scale, the private security industry is ideally placed to act as force multipliers in crime prevention and in so doing contribute to the achievement of SDG16, especially in times and context of an emergency. As part of the lockdown regulations, the Government classified private security services as essential services, which meant that the sector could continue operating during the hard lockdown to perform guarding and other duties. The private security sector did not have any directive from government to assist or support law enforcement efforts.

The Philippines

On 16 March 2020, President Duterte declared a State of Calamity throughout the Philippines due to Covid-19 through Proclamation No. 929. Accordingly, the period would extend six months and it imposed an Enhanced Community Quarantine (ECQ) throughout Luzon (the main Philippine island) until 12 April 2020 (Republic of the Philippines 2020). The President tasked the executive and health secretaries and all heads of departments to issue guidelines on the quarantine, which included strict home isolation that limited activities to accessing necessities. Similar measures imposed in Metro Manila the previous week reportedly failed to limit public activities (Republic of the Philippines 2020b). The Philippine Congress passed the *Bayanihan Heal as One Act* on 24 March 2020, giving the President exceptional powers, such as taking control of privately owned hospitals, to respond to the Covid-19 pandemic. In September 2020, President Duterte extended the State of Calamity for one year until 12 September 2021 through Proclamation No. 1021 (Republic of the Philippines 2020a).

President Duterte directed all law enforcement agencies, with the support from the armed forces of the Philippines (AFP), to undertake all necessary measures to ensure peace and order in affected areas. In a media statement, President Duterte assured citizens that although there would be more police officers and soldiers visible in the streets, Luzon was not under martial rule (Republic of the Philippines 2020c). The President regarded the Philippines to be 'at war against a vicious and invisible enemy...' and addressing the public, further stated, 'In this extraordinary war, we are all soldiers' (Republic of the Philippines 2020c).

The AFP were not deployed with policing powers in law enforcement capabilities, but to perform complementary roles in various joint operations and the enforcement of curfews related to ECQ remained the responsibility of the Philippine National Police (PNP) and the local government units (LGUs). The AFP personnel supported the PNP at selected checkpoints, public markets, etc., and at the request of the LGUs. The military was moreover employed in logistic and humanitarian capacities to transport protective equipment, medical equipment, testing kits and frontline personnel in the cities and across the various islands of the Philippines. The Philippine Navy used assets to facilitate repatriation efforts and AFP engineering teams were involved in building 29 Emergency Quarantine Facilities to support hospitals and health facilities with inadequate rooms. A number of AFP military kitchen trucks were deployed as 'mobile kitchens' serving the homeless in the Metro Manila (OHCHR 2020).

Similar to South Africa, the UN High Commissioner for Human Rights raised concern about the measures used in the Philippines to enforce lockdown regulations and curfews as being 'highly militarised'. Efforts to contain the spread of Covid-19 led to the arrest of 120 000 people for curfew violations in the first month and a half of the ECQ (United Nations 2020). Since the start of the ECQ, various cases of abuse were reported including a barangay (village) official who placed five youths in a dog cage for violating the curfew (Wurth 2020) and a police officer who fatally shot a former army corporal for supposed ECQ violations (Ferreras 2020).

Shortly after the proclamation of the ECQ, President Duterte told police and military officers to shoot 'troublemakers' protesting during the quarantine period (Amnesty International 2020). The President further warned citizens not to intimidate or challenge the Government, telling them, 'You will lose' (Capatides 2020). However, the PNP Chief later clarified that the officers understood that they were not actually being instructed to kill troublemakers and that 'Probably the president just overemphasized on the implementing the law in this time of crisis' (Capatides 2020). In July 2020, the PNP started to go house-to-house to find people with Covid-19 symptoms and ask neighbours to report on those believed to be infected (Olanday 2020). The PNP issued a directive on 22 April 2020 to reiterate the implementation of Human Rights-Based Policing during the ECQ, including that there must be strict monitoring and evaluation of the behaviour of troops shifting to 'arrest' mode and that a maximum tolerance policy should be exercised (OHCHR 2020). Despite various contraventions by the AFP and PNP, an independent opinion survey recorded high public satisfaction ratings of government agencies' response to Covid-19 in Metro Manila. The survey showed a 90% and 88% satisfaction rating for the AFP and PNP respectively (RLR Research and Analysis Inc 2020).

In the Philippines, the role of private security remained limited, but more pronounced than in the case of South Africa. In March 2020, the PNP announced protocols authorising security agencies and guards to act as force multipliers to secure their posted areas during the ECQ in Luzon, especially when such businesses were closed (Pulta 2020). This authorisation is of significance given that the size of the private security industry is estimated at 1,675 private security agencies operating employing 670,000 security guards (Business World Online 2014). These agencies outnumber that of the AFP (130,000 officers) and the PNP (160,000 officers) (Tan 2020). The Private Security Industry Act, 2021 provides that the PNP shall excise general supervision of all private security agencies (Philippine Congress 2021).

The United Kingdom

The Prime Minister of the UK did not invoke emergency powers under the Civil Contingencies Act, 2004, but instead used the Public Health (Control of Disease) Act, 1984, and the new Coronavirus Act, 2020, to address the spread of Covid-19 (Bennett Institute for Public Policy 2020). The Coronavirus Act, 2020, was processed as emergency legislation introduced to Parliament on 19 March 2020, and passed by the House of Commons on 23 March 2020 without a vote, and the House of Lords on 25 March 2020. The Act received Royal Assent on the same day and enabled an emergency response to the Covid-19 pandemic that is set to remain in force for two years, unless the Government suspends it earlier. The first lockdown came into effect on 23 March 2020. The Health Protection (Coronavirus, Restrictions) (England) Regulations 2020, or the lockdown rules, were promulgated by the Secretary of State for Health under the emergency powers available in the Public Health (Control of Disease) Act, 1984, on 26 March 2020, and was not subjected to Parliamentary scrutiny.

Schedule 21 of the Coronavirus Act, 2020, and the Health Protection (Coronavirus, Restrictions) (England) Regulations 2020 provide various responsibilities and powers to the police forces across the UK. While the Act empowers the police to support public health services in testing and treatment of individuals, Section 8 of the Regulations empowers 'relevant persons' (including police) to take action against those deemed to violate the lockdown restrictions, such as gatherings and restrictions on movement. As per Schedule 21 of the Coronavirus Act, 2020, the police may arrest a person 'failing without reasonable excuse to comply with any direction, reasonable instruction, requirement of restriction'. However, this only applies to a 'potentially infectious person' and in cases where a public health officer requests the police for such support. According to the College of Policing, the role of officers 'in most cases, is to standby and prevent a breach of the peace while health officers perform their public duty' (College of Policing 2020). The Act empowers the police to issue fines of up to £1,000 for main offences. According to a report by the National Police Chiefs' Council (NPCC), a total of 42,675 fixed penalty notices were issued by forces in England and Wales between 27 March 2020 and 17 January 2021 (Gillespie 2021).

Little evidence exists of significant police abuses, in terms of brutality, during the lockdown enforcement. The majority of issues arose straight after the start of the lockdown due to confusion around the interpretation of regulations. The lack of clarity led to the fragmented implementation of the lockdown rules by different police forces countrywide. One of the most problematic interpretations was that the guidance/rules restricted 'non-essential' travel (which it did not) and a number of police forces reportedly set up roadblocks to question motorists on whether the journey was 'essential' (Joint Committee on Human Rights 2020). There was also confusion over whether the police could or should question people on their movements and request to justify themselves. According to the Joint Standing Committee on Human Rights, 'the regulations have fundamentally, if temporally, altered the relationship between the police and the citizens and perhaps even between citizens' (Joint Committee on Human Rights 2020). The Committee raised further concerns over the highly intrusive nature of the police's questioning of citizens on whether they had a 'reasonable excuse' for leaving their homes. Subsequently, the NPCC and College of Policing issued additional guidance to clarify that the Regulations do not give police the power to 'stop and account'. This point was emphasised in early April 2020, when a woman refused to give police officers her name, address or reasons for travel. The police subsequently charged her under the Coronavirus Act, 2020, and kept her in custody for two days. A Magistrates Court convicted her and issued a £660 fine. However, the British Transport Police conducted a review with the Crown Prosecution Service establishing that the police had charged her under the incorrect section of the Coronavirus Act, 2020, and stated that the conviction would be set aside (Dearden 2020).

At the start of the lockdown in March 2020, the UK Prime Minister indicated that the armed forces were ready to 'backfill' if the police were struck by staff shortages, but only 'under a reasonable worst case scenario' (Reuters 2020). This was met with heavy criticism from the NPCC, highlighting the unique role of policing and careful consideration should be given to any form of military support (Dodd 2020). Equally, Members of Parliament sought clarity on the Prime Minister's proposal to deploy the military to support the police. It was latter clarified that the military would perform duties such as office roles, to enable police officers to enforce the new lockdown rules, and that the military would not participate in law enforcement operations. During the initial stages of the pandemic, a team from the Royal Logistics Corps assisted the police with the distribution of personal protective equipment (PPE) up until the establishment of the National Police Central Logistics Hub. By March 2021, this was the only way in which the military assisted the police (UK Government 2020).

On 18 March 2020, the Defence Secretary announced the establishment of a Covid Support Force (CSF) to contribute to public services in the Government's Covid-19 response efforts. In January 2021, the armed forces had 4,670 personnel committed to 56 ongoing tasks in support of 13 government departments and almost 10,000 additional personnel on high alert for rapid deployment (Wallace 2021). The armed forces helped to build Nightingale hospitals and, according to the Defence Secretary, distributed more that 6 million PPE items to hospitals (Wallace 2021). Consultants, clinicians, nurses and trainees from the Defence Medical Services assisted the NHS in hospitals. Personnel from the Defence Science and Technology Labs were involved in several Covid-19 related projects supporting the Government's understanding of the virus and analysts from Defence Intelligence studied the ways in which Covid-19 spreads (Wallace 2021). The armed forces were also expected to support the logistics and supply chains for vaccinations. During an oral statement in Parliament on 12 January 2021, the Defence Secretary stated, 'Defence's contribution to the Covid response now represents the most significant domestic resilient operation in peacetime' and that the armed forces 'might not have been on the frontline of this particular fight but we (armed forces) are with them "in the trenches"...' (Wallace 2021).

As part of the lockdown enforcement, security operatives were considered critical workers when providing critical security provisions in hospitals, social care, the courts, government estate buildings, as well as key supermarkets/food supply chains, the transport network and critical national infrastructure and utilities. Further thereto, the Home Office provided that roles essential to supporting law and order, or which limit any further likely pressures on the police or national emergency services, were considered critical (SIA 2021a). According to Security Industry Authority (SIA), the UK had a total of 375,111 approved licence holders and 833 approved contractors, of which the majority were operating in the security guarding sector (786 contractors) (SIA 2021b). At 31 March 2021, the total strength of the 43 police forces in England and Wales was 135,301 full time officers (Allen & Harding 2021). In some metropolitan areas, the discrepancy is particularly pronounced as in, for example, London's Oxford Street where private security personnel outnumber police officers by 18 to one (Vinci 2020).

Parliaments' varying capacity during Covid-19

During the Covid-19 pandemic, states took various legislative and policy routes in dealing with the Covid-19 pandemic and while there is no 'correct' approach, there are good practices that have been observed globally, including 'legal certainty, transparency in decision-making, clarity in communication, an early reaction, and co-ordinated strategy' (Grogan 2020). However, these were lacking in many instances as parliaments were often side-lined in governments' Covid-19 responses. The side-lining of parliament poses a significant threat in the form of executive over-reach or dominance. This was the case in a number of countries where Ministers used secondary legislation, also known as 'subordinate legislation', in the form of Regulations (also known as Statutory Instruments). This was prominent in both South Africa and the UK, where lockdown restrictions were enforced through regulations not subject to parliamentary scrutiny. In itself, secondary legislation does not normally necessitate parliamentary scrutiny as it contains specific areas of implementation and is often only tabled in parliaments for information, not for consideration. However, when secondary legislation restricts normal freedoms in a fundamental way, scrutiny becomes vital and has the potential to impact negatively on parliaments' legislative function.

The internal arrangements of parliaments had a further impact on its core functions, specifically in the immediate period after Covid-19 emergency declarations. Many parliaments essentially suspended its functions, because of physical barriers (social distancing and limitations of movement) and technological challenges (where virtual platforms were not developed). This forced innovation and the setup of virtual platforms in order to resume oversight functions. However, a lack of activity by parliaments in conjunction with executive overreach provided a poor foundation for effective representation of the citizenry.

South Africa

The Disaster Management Act, 2002, bestowed wide-ranging powers on the Minister of Cooperative Governance and Traditional Affairs as the custodian of the Act, amongst which is to promulgate secondary legislation (Regulations) in order to release any available resources of the national government. As mentioned earlier, the promulgated Regulations to the Act enabled the law enforcement role of the SAPS and SANDF. The initial hard lockdown was only for a period of 21 days, but was extended numerous times and remained in place by March 2021, a full year after first being implemented. The alternative governmental response would have been to declare a state of emergency through the State of Emergency Act (64 of 1997), which allows greater parliamentary oversight. However, as argued by a Constitutional expert, a state of emergency would have been a radical step and would have allowed the Government to derogate from most of the human rights as enshrined in the Constitution and could encourage further authoritarian behaviour (De Vos 2020).

Amid the looming national lockdown, Parliament announced the indefinite suspension of the programme of both its Houses from 19 March 2020 as a precautionary measure to limit the spread of Covid-19 (Parliament RSA 2020c). MPs continued to work in their respective constituencies from 23 March to 13 April 2020 as the lockdown regulations classified MPs as those performing essential services. In a media statement, Parliament 'reminded' MPs that 'the responsibility to conduct oversight is, therefore, not limited to committee meetings' (Parliament RSA 2020d). Parliament remained closed to the public from 18 March 2020 and arranged to reduce the number of staff members in the precinct in line with lockdown regulations (Parliament RSA 2020c). By March 2021, the majority of staff had not yet returned to the precinct and staff continue to make use of remote working arrangements.

The suspension of Parliament's programme elicited heavy criticism from various quarters and the institution was accused of abandoning its Constitutional mandate. Opposition political parties and NGOs made several efforts to increase oversight. Immediately after the announcement of the hard lockdown, the Parliamentary Leader of the official opposition party *(Democratic Alliance)* wrote to the Speaker requesting the establishment of an ad hoc committee to conduct oversight of the executive and the 'protection of civil liberties' during the Covid-19 lockdown (Parliament RSA 2020e). However, Parliament denied the request stating that the mandate was too broad and that it 'would not be feasible to expect a single ad hoc committee to perform it' (Parliament RSA 2020e). In addition, Parliament stated that it covered oversight and accountability work done by existing parliamentary committees and MPs, 'in line with their areas of specialisation' (Parliament RSA 2020e).

It was only in April 2020 that the Presiding Officers announced the resumption of Parliament's programme (Parliament RSA 2020a). In an effort to prioritise Parliament's oversight function, the Presiding Officers cancelled the leave period for MPs scheduled for 28 April to 04 May 2020 and announced that it would prioritise a schedule of virtual meetings for oversight of government departments driving Covid-19 response measures. Parliament further stated that these committees were required to intensify their oversight engagements, particularly on Covid-19 matters, and should conduct joint meetings. Curiously, Parliament stated

> In performing its constitutional obligations during this period, Parliament must not be seen as interfering with the responsibility of the Executive to implement measures for which the National State of Disaster has been declared. It remains the responsibility of the Executive to deliver much-needed services to save the lives of individuals. However, holding such meetings, specifically to conduct oversight over implementation of the lockdown regulations, may require the Executive to attend briefings. This could risk taking them away from their extremely critical function of managing measures to combat spread of COVID-19 and preserving life. (Parliament RSA 2020d).

Such comments could be interpreted as to discourage calling the executive to account before parliamentary committees and seen as a contradiction to the institution's oversight function.

During the closure, Parliament benchmarked best practices by other legislatures and put in place the necessary information and communication technology infrastructure to ensure its readiness for virtual meetings. In addition, Parliament adopted guidelines and rules on how to conduct virtual meetings and voting in both Houses. According to health protocols and observing social distancing, 166 members from a total of 400 members (42%), were allowed to attend House sittings in person.

The National Assembly had its first hybrid sitting on 27 May 2020, during which Ministers and Deputy Ministers in the Cluster responsible for the Government's response to Covid-19 responded to written and oral questions. The National Council of Provinces held its first exclusively virtual sitting on 2 June 2020.

Upon the resumption of Parliament's programme, it continued its legislative function during the lockdown period through hybrid sessions. A secure online voting system had not been developed, but the revised Parliamentary Rules on virtual meetings provided for the following:

- Members shall be entitled to cast their votes either electronically, by voice or by having their vote recorded by their respective whips.
- The procedure to be followed is predetermined by the Speaker and directives are announced in the meeting by the Presiding Officer or Chairperson of a committee.
- Only members who are present when a vote is called shall be permitted to vote (both physically and remotely).
- The results of a vote are announced and, where possible, the names of members and how they voted are recorded in the Minutes of Proceedings.
- Members must ensure that their votes are correctly recorded.

In terms of Covid-19 specific legislation, Parliament only dealt with budget-related legislation that reprioritised state funds for the Government's response to Covid-19 during 2020. The Minister of

Finance introduced the Adjustments Appropriation Bill on 22 June 2020 and the Division of Revenue Amendment Bill on 23 June 2020. The Bills passed through both Houses of Parliament on 04 August 2020. These Bills allocated significant additional funds to the SANDF and SAPS to execute their respective law enforcement operations. Parliament also passed the Disaster Management Tax Relief Bill, 2020 and the Disaster Management Tax Relief Administration Bill, 2020.

The Disaster Management Act, 2002, and the associated Regulations did not require any involvement by Parliament in its approval, extension or its termination. Parliament did not consider any legislation related to the Government's response to Covid-19, leaving all policy decisions to the executive. Between March 2020 and March 2021, the Government extended the national lockdown 16 times and gazetted 27 lockdown regulations, 20 guidelines and notices and 179 directives. On 19 February 2021, an opposition MP (Dr Groenewald from the Freedom Front Plus) introduced the Disaster Management Amendment Bill (B2-2021) into Parliament as a private member's bill. The Amendment Bill calls for greater parliamentary scrutiny in the declaration of and restriction imposed by a disaster in that Parliament, with a 60% majority, must approve the extension thereof beyond an initial period of 21 days. The Bill was referred to the Portfolio Committee on Cooperative Government and Traditional Affairs and is under consideration by the National Assembly. Once Parliament resumed its programme, in April 2020, it had well developed internal arrangements to fulfil its core functions. As such, it is evident that Parliament's representative and legislative functions caught up through technological innovations in establishing functional hybrid sittings. However, the lack of scrutiny on disaster management-related legislation remains a challenge for effective representation of the citizenry.

The Philippines

On 08 March 2020, President Duterte declared a state of public health emergency throughout the Philippines through Proclamation No. 922 and imposed several restrictions on public movement in Metro Manila (National Capital Region). On 16 March 2020, restrictions were increased prior to the declaration of a state of calamity (Proclamation No. 929). On 21 March 2020, President Duterte issued Proclamation No. 933 calling the Congress of the Philippines to a special session on 23 March 2020. This was to authorise emergency presidential powers to deal with the Covid-19 pandemic, including allowing Congress to utilise funds in order to strengthen the governmental response against Covid-19 (Proclamation No. 933 s. 2020). On 23 March 2020, the House of Representatives almost unanimously approved the Bayanihan to Heal as One Act, 2020 (Bayanihan 1) with 284 affirmative votes, nine negative votes, and no abstention. Due to the urgency of the Covid-19 pandemic, the House of Representatives approved on second and third readings without undergoing the normal three-day rule between approvals (Cervantes 2020).

The session was the first virtual sitting in the history of Congress and Members voted through telephone, text, messaging apps and videoconference tools. The chamber allowed only 20 House Members, aside from the Speaker, to be physically present at the Plenary Hall, while other MPs joined the deliberations through teleconferencing (Philippine House of Representatives 2020). In a press release, the Speaker lauded the unprecedented cooperation between the executive and legislative to pass the Bayanihan 1 (Philippine House of Representatives 2020).

The Philippine House of Representatives suspended its programme straight after the approval of the Bayanihan 1 from 23 March to 12 April 2020 to prevent the spread of Covid-19. The House implemented a rotating skeletal workforce for the duration of the suspension. Committee hearings, briefings and conferences were allowed in the House of Representative to address the spread of Covid-19 and mitigate its impact. The Philippine Senate had already suspended regular session on 09 March 2020 and went on recess until 04 May 2020. However, sessions were held to approve the Bayanihan 1 during the recess. The transition to a hybrid set-up seemed to be seamless and both Houses adapted with apparent ease. As a safeguard against executive overreach, the Bayanihan 1 required the President to submit detailed weekly reports to Congress on all acts performed by the Executive branch of government related to Covid-19, especially on the use of emergency funds. The Act also included a sunset clause, allowing the Act to remain in force for only three months and expired in June 2020 (Atienza 2021).

Subsequent legislation, the Bayanihan to Recover as One Act, 2020 (Bayanihan 2), extended the presidential emergency powers granted by the Bayanihan 1. Similarly, it specified that the President must, this time, submit monthly (instead of weekly) reports on the use of funds to both Congress and the Commission on Audit. The Act went through the regular legislative process being filed on 03 June 2020, but only approved on 20 August 2020. The Bayanihan 2 lapsed on 19 December 2020 when Congress adjourned its sessions for the year (Gotinga 2020a). The Bayanihan 3 (Bayanihan to Arise as One Act) was filed in February 2021 (and passed by the House of Representatives on 01 June 2021. As of October 2021, Congress has not yet passed Bayanihan 3).

Through the easy transition to virtual and hybrid sittings, the representative function continued. However, the speed at which both Houses approved the Bayanihan 1 arguably detracted from representation, as its content could not be fully unpacked. Successive legislation followed the regular process and ensured sufficient legislative scrutiny (despite the extension of extraordinary presidential powers).

The United Kingdom

The UK's 'state of emergency' was not called in law, thus not through existing emergency legislative provisions such as the Civil Contingencies Act, 2004. The Government relied on the Public Health (Control of Disease) Act, 1984 to draft and promulgate the Health Protection (Coronavirus, Restrictions) (England) Regulations, 2020, which came into effect on 26 March 2020 giving legal effect to the lockdown announced by the Prime Minister on 23 March 2020. The Regulations represented the most far-reaching restrictions on individuals since the Defence Regulations made during the Second World War (Joint Committee on Human Rights 2020). Further, the Act involved the largest expansion of executive power seen in peacetime (Parkinson 2020). Despite this, the Regulations had not been subjected to any parliamentary scrutiny because the Secretary of State for Health, under emergency powers, promulgated it. The original set of regulations have since been subject to an ongoing judicial review that claims that it exceeded the scope of power given by Parliament under the 1984 Act (Parkinson 2020).

The Regulations, which must ordinarily be approved by both Houses of Parliament within 21 days, was introduced pursuant to an urgent procedure and thus bypassed the approval process. Between January 2020 and February 2021, the Government had laid 379 Covid-19 related statutory instruments before the UK Parliament of which 93 required approval from both Houses of Parliament. However, 81 of these were made using urgent powers, thus foregoing Parliamentary approval (Hansard Society 2021).

The Commons Select Committee on Public Administration published a scathing report in September 2020 on the Government's approach to legislation, specifically the use of secondary legislation (legislative instruments) to regulate and enforce the lockdown. The use of the urgent procedure had impacted the timelines of parliamentary debate, as the report stated,

> By the time that the Health Protection (Coronavirus, Restrictions) (England) (Amendment) (No. 3) Regulations 2020 were debated, the Health Protection (Coronavirus, Restrictions) (England) (Amendment) (No. 4) Regulations 2020 were already in force and the Amendment (No.4) regulations were never even debated in the House of Commons,

although they were debated in the House of Lords (Commons Select Committee Public Administration 2020).

The report further expressed concern in the fact that there is no mechanism to amend secondary legislation (Commons Select Committee Public Administration 2020).

The primary legislative response was through the Coronavirus Act, 2020, which was taken through both Houses of Parliament in only four days (including the first reading) without a division being called, as political parties had agreed to fast track the emergency legislation and forgo the division lobbies. Chapter 4 of the Act sets out points of interest to Parliament for the first six-month Parliamentary review. Additionally, Parliament passed the Contingencies Fund Act, 2020, to increase funding of the Covid-19 response. The limited number of primary legislation stands in stark contrast to that of secondary legislation.

The House of Commons went on a month-long Easter recess on 25 March 2020 (after passing the Coronavirus Act, 2020) during which work on Parliament's technological capabilities continued, including the development of a system that enabled MPs to vote remotely using an online portal (Lilly 2020a). Towards the end of March 2020, MPs were calling for a virtual House of Commons to be established to scrutinise the Government's response to Covid-19. On 14 April 2020, the Speaker put forward detailed plans for remote participation in temporary 'hybrid' parliamentary proceedings, to which MPs agreed. After the May recess, the temporary 'hybrid' proceedings lapsed and MPs had to return to the Commons on 02 June 2020. The House agreed to allow MPs unable to attend Parliament for medical reasons to participate remotely in questions and statements, but could not participate remotely in debates on legislation (Lilly 2020).

On 16 June 2020, the Speaker announced that divisions in the House of Commons would be conducted in the division lobbies using an electronic pass-reader system. When a division begins, MPs should go to Westminster Hall and join one of two queues (whichever is shortest). As MPs pass through the required voting lobby (either 'Aye' or 'No') they should tap their pass on the pass-reader to register their vote. On 3 November 2020, the House further extended proxy voting to any MP that does not wish to vote in person for medical or public health reasons relating to the pandemic. Around 170 MPs made use of proxies. By March 2021, there was still no provision for MPs unable to attend the chamber for medical reasons to take part in debates on legislation. When the House of Commons was recalled (on 30 December 2020), MPs agreed to extend remote participation in proceedings in the Chamber to all MPs. The House of Lords adopted a more favourable stance towards virtual proceedings. Within a few days of returning from the Easter recess, all forms of business were being carried out virtually (Lilly 2020). Throughout April and May, more forms of business were conducted remotely, including debates on primary and secondary legislation. In June 2020, the House decided to move to hybrid proceedings, with up to 30 peers being allowed in the chamber at any one time. At the same time, remote voting was introduced, with the first remote vote taking place on 15 June. Outside of the chamber, many Lords committees have been conducting hybrid or remote evidence sessions (Lilly 2020).

Representation provides for interplay between Parliament and the citizenry, while an open legislative process fosters transparency in the rule of law. The excessive use of secondary legislation by the Government in its Covid-19 response, side-lined Parliament's legislative function and, as such, jeopardised its representative function. The reversion of the hybrid sitting arrangements in June 2020, could have further excluded full representation in the business of the House.

Exercising parliamentary oversight of the security sector during Covid-19

During the initial phases of the Covid-19 pandemic, the normal functioning of parliaments, notably their oversight function, were negatively affected. This impediment to parliamentary oversight coincided with noteworthy security sector deployments in many states. In South Africa, the Philippines and the UK, parliaments were unable to execute in-depth scrutiny over the initial utilisation of the security sector by the executive. However, an important indicator of parliamentary resilience is found in the question: Once parliaments resumed executing their functions again following the initial Covid-19 outbreak, how did they apply the key oversight tools and functions to ensure accountability and transparency of the security sector? An analysis of these trends in South Africa, the Philippines and the UK parliament reveals varied outcomes. The UK Parliament launched several in-depth investigations into the use of the security sector during Covid-19, as did the Parliament of South Africa albeit in a less structured manner. The Philippines Parliament also resumed its normal functions, but in the context of significant powers handed to the executive, oversight of the security sector was comparatively subdued. The work of the various parliaments also revealed varied levels of transparency in security sector matters which is a key requirement for building not only a transparent security sector, but also transparent parliaments. Transparency in all cases were adversely affected during the initial Covid-19 outbreak response period, but recovered to varying degrees as parliaments resumed their functions. The two sections which follow expands on security sector accountability and transparency in the three case studies.

Security sector transparency during Covid-19

South Africa

In line with global trends, the relatively slow uptake of virtual platforms by the Parliament of South Africa amid the initial lockdown period inhibited transparency of the security sector. Parliamentary tools for oversight were not utilised during this initial period, which is of specific concern given the amplified role of the security forces during this period. However, over time, a significant improvement in oversight is noticeable and tools were used more effectively.

South Africa's initial hard lockdown commenced on 26 March 2020 which coincided with the suspension of parliamentary activities. *Parliamentary debates* around the security sector did not take place during this period, specifically at committee level.[3] Parliament's two defence committees held only one meeting between 11 March and 1 May 2020, during a period in which the entire SANDF was placed on standby and an average of 8,091 personnel were deployed daily (PMG 2021a). While the meeting dealt with the deployment of the military and complaints of misconduct, the general lack of defence committee meetings between March and May 2020 hindered transparency around initial deployments. The Portfolio Committee on Police similarly did not meet from 11 March until 29 April 2020, when it considered the police's management of the nationwide lockdown. Following the resumption of virtual committee meetings, debate around the security sector increased significantly. The two defence committees held a total of 36 meetings between May and December 2020, while the Portfolio Committee on Police held 24 over the same period. It should be noted that these were not specific to Covid-19, but included elements thereof. These figures compared favourably to previous years, an important factor in the maintenance of continued security sector transparency.

In the absence of committee activity during the initial lockdown period, *parliamentary questions* offered an alternative avenue to ensure continued transparency around the security sector. However, the initial inactivity of Parliament was also reflected in terms of questions to security sector ministries. For example, between 13 March and 3 June 2020, no questions were posed to

---

[3] All information on the regularity of parliamentary committee meetings were obtained from the Parliamentary Monitoring Group at https://pmg.org.za/.

the Minister of Defence.[4] Over the same period, only 10 questions were posed to the Minister of Police. There was an increase in questions posed over the remainder of 2020, with 59 questions to the Minister of Police and 46 to the Minister of Defence, many of which related to the use of the security forces during Covid-19 and signalling a return of transparency as a result of parliamentary activity. While the use of questions resumed, the Covid-19 pandemic had a devastating impact on the use of *oversight visits* as an oversight tool due to national travel restrictions. The two defence committees managed to conduct two oversight visits. They held an in-person workshop with SANDF commanders on the organisational structure in October 2020 and conducted a visit to selected military units and border deployment areas in November 2020. The Covid-19 SANDF deployments were not central to the visit. The official report for the oversight was not yet formally adopted and tabled by the beginning of March 2021, which in regards to the maintenance of transparency, is concerning given the need for timely release of information (PMG 2021b). The Portfolio Committee on Police conducted no oversight visits between March 2020 and March 2021.

The use of *external audits* by Parliament has improved significantly over the last two decades, adding to the transparency of most sectors. The Auditor-General conducted a series of Covid-19 related expenditure investigations on selected government departments, including the Department of Defence (DOD). The initial audit did not include the police, thus no external audit was conducted on Covid-19 related spending. The Portfolio Committee on Defence and Military Veterans, held two meetings in February 2021 on the audit outcomes of a special investigation into the DOD's procurement of Covid-19 medication from Cuba. The medication was not cleared for import and use by the South African Health Products Regulatory Authority and the procurement allegedly did not follow the correct procurement procedures (SABC News 2021). While the use of external audit provides a form of *in-depth inquiry*, parliamentary rules also allow for the creation of ad hoc or sub-committees. It was already noted that a proposed Covid-19 ad hoc committee was not agreed to. Similarly, no sub-committees of the defence or police portfolio committees were established to look specifically into the use of the security forces during Covid-19. Furthermore, there was no cooperation between the police and defence committees in Parliament, despite the SANDF being deployed in cooperation with the police.

In addition to the use of oversight tools, the *transparency of parliaments* themselves are crucial to boost security sector transparency. The Parliament of South Africa has a good track record in terms of the openness of its oversight of the security sector. Except for the Joint Standing Committee on Intelligence, which holds closed meetings, defence and police committees do not generally hold closed meetings and no closed meetings were held between March 2020 and March 2021. Furthermore, Parliament publishes regular media information alerts which are available on the parliamentary website. Between May 2020 and March 2021, several press releases per month from the police and defence committees were issued (Parliament RSA 2021). Where Parliament arguably falls short in its contribution to security sector transparency is in the timely and open publication of information. This represents a historic problem at Parliament that continued during the Covid-19 period (Janse van Rensburg 2019: 121). Defence and police committee meeting minutes are not available on the parliamentary website. Rather, the Parliamentary Monitoring Group (PMG), an NGO, is the only institution that keeps updated, searchable electronic records of parliamentary committee meetings. While much of PMG's information is freely available, access to the police and defence committee minutes requires payment. Furthermore, Parliament's website does not provide an easily searchable platform to search for security-sector parliamentary questions, tabled reports and even House debates. The Covid-19 pandemic and uptake of virtual committee

---

[4] All information on the regularity of parliamentary questions were obtained from the Parliamentary Monitoring Group at https://pmg.org.za/.

sittings did, however, have a positive outcome in terms of transparency. All virtual meetings were live-streamed on Parliament's YouTube channel and remain uploaded for easy access.

The Philippines

The Philippine Congress passed the Bayanihan Heal as One Act, 2020 at speed in March 2020, which gave the President wide-ranging power to respond to Covid-19. The second and third readings were completed without subjection to the normal three-day rule between approvals, resulting in limited opportunity for in-depth *debate* on its content. Crucially, the lack of debate around the legislation likewise excluded thorough engagement on the potential utilisation of the security sector in response to the pandemic. Additionally, Congress went into recess right after passing the Act until mid-April 2020, which further frustrated continuity in oversight over the Government's Covid-19 response plan and implementation. The approach to the Bayanihan Recover as One Act (Bayanihan 2) was also rushed. The President had certified the bill as urgent, which lifted the three-day rule between the second and third readings, again limiting any debate around security sector utilisation despite the Act extending the President's emergency powers to the end of June 2021.

As Parliament resumed, debate around the security sector in the immediate post-lockdown phase was largely facilitated through committee activity. The Defeat Covid-19 Ad-Hoc Committee (DCC) was established to address all matters relating to the appropriate government response to Covid-19 and to curb its effects on the economy and the public. The DCC consisted of 10 MPs and was divided into five separate focus clusters, including a Peace and Order Cluster. Debate at this Cluster was, however, limited, with little focus on the utilisation of the security sector. On 11 May 2020, the Cluster considered the draft House Bill 6676 on prohibiting the discrimination against persons who are confirmed, suspect, probable and recovered cases of Covid-19, repatriated Filipinos, healthcare workers, responders and service workers and providing penalties for violation thereof. The use of the DCC therefore did not fill the need for inquiry into security sector matters related to Covid-19 deployments. Rather, the Parliament conducted *special inquiries* through a series of House-approved investigations.

Section 21 Article VI of the Philippine Constitution provides that the House of Representatives, or any of its committees, may conduct inquiries in aid of legislation in accordance with the Rules (House of Representatives Rules). Such investigations are called through House Resolutions and form part of the legislative process. This mechanism has been used during the Covid-19 pandemic to request investigations into various issues, notably human rights violations by law enforcement officials, including the following:

- HR826: Directing the House Committee on Human Rights to conduct an investigation on the series of mass arrests and other human rights violations by law enforcers since the implementation of the enhanced community quarantine, and to recommend measures to ensure the protection of the civil and political rights of Filipinos in the midst of the Covid-19 pandemic. The first reading was on 11 May 2020 and referred to the Defeat Covid-19 Ad-Hoc Committee on 27 May 2020 and was still pending by March 2021 (House Resolution 826, 2020).
- HR832: Urging the Committee on Human Rights to investigate the human rights violations perpetrated during the implementation of the community quarantine. The first reading was on 11 May 2020 and referred to the Defeat Covid-19 Ad-Hoc Committee on 27 May 2020 and was still pending by March 2021 (House Resolution 832, 2020).
- HR1036: Directing the Committee on Human Rights to conduct an inquiry on the extrajudicial killings and human rights violations against farmers during the community

quarantine. The first reading was on 28 July 2020 and referred to the Defeat Covid-19 Ad-Hoc Committee on 11 August 2020 and was still pending by March 2021.

Although the abovementioned resolutions called for the investigations to be conducted by the Committee on Human Rights, the Defeat Covid-19 Ad-Hoc Committee dealt with all issues related to Covid-19. The investigations showed good use of a unique parliamentary oversight tool to ensure transparency. Arguably, the timespan of these pending investigations impacted negatively on both transparency and accountability of the security sector and the timely finalisation of these investigations could have improved the manner in which law enforcers interacted with the public during the community quarantine.

Debate around the security sector ultimately resumed with the resumption of normal committee activity. The Philippine House of Representatives has two standing committees focussed on the security sector, namely the Standing Committee on National Defence and Security and the Standing Committee on Public Order and Safety, including a Subcommittee on Police Administration. These committees met regularly up until the national lockdown and resumed business in May 2020. Both Committees had meetings on significant issues affecting the security sector. Further, the two Committees had regular joint meetings on legislation affecting the security sector, such as the Anti-Terrorism Act, 2020. The 'committee reports' or outcomes of committee meetings are legislation and amended legislation, which must be operationalised and to which the executive must account, thus it provides a high level of transparency. The lack of detailed committee minutes on the parliamentary website does, however, complicate an analysis of the depth of inquiry of the security sector by these committees.

The use of *external audit* held further potential to aid transparency around the security sector's utilisation during Covid-19. In July 2020, a Senate Resolution (No. 479, 2020) urged the Commission on Audit (COA) to conduct a special audit on Covid-19 related spending, loans and donations under the Bayanihan 1. The Act allowed the urgent procurement of commodities and services deemed essential in the Covid-19 response, such as PPE and laboratory equipment, and exempted these procurements for the required bidding process. The Resolution highlighted various allegations of overpricing of emergency items that had surfaced and requested that the COA must present the findings before Congress starts its deliberation of the 2021 budget for the audit findings to guide legislators in exercising the power of the purse (Congress of the Philippines 2020). The President's weekly reports contained information on spending but there was not sufficient detail on procurement and suppliers (Gotinga 2020). Despite the COA's capacity having been hampered by Covid-19 restrictions, the Commission confirmed that an audit project was ongoing and that it will employ artificial intelligence to sift through government documents faster (Lalu 2020). Nonetheless, delays in the finalisation of audits by the COA limited the immediate impact on transparency around procurement, including in the security sector. Parliament's contribution to transparency will further be highly dependent on how well it engages with the final COA findings and how it holds the security sector to account.

In addition to the use of oversight tools, the *transparency of parliaments* themselves are crucial to boost security sector transparency. The Philippine Congress fosters openness of its oversight of the security sector through its digital platforms, including live streams, websites and Facebook and Twitter accounts, all of which are up-to-date and current. Most of these have been active since the start of the 17th Congress in 2016. The House of Representatives publishes regular press releases that capture relevant information in an easily understandable format. The website further offers access to timely and open information on daily committee business as well as plenary sessions. However, detailed minutes of committee meetings are not available, but substituted with Daily Committee Bulletins that provide an account of the most salient matters raised in committee meetings. This resource enables the public to follow the business and discussions of committees.

The United Kingdom

The UK Parliament has a strong culture of transparency over the security sector when considering the use of available oversight tools. As with most parliaments, the Covid-19 pandemic forced the temporary suspension of parliamentary programmes, which coincided with the Parliament's Easter recess. Nonetheless, the UK Parliament approved the Coronavirus Act, 2020, at speed and without voting in order to fast track the operationalisation of the legislation. The emergency created by Covid-19 made lengthy parliamentary *debate* impractical, which is unfortunate given that thorough debate could have eliminated the initial confusion around the application of the Coronavirus Act. Crucially, the lack of debate around the legislation also excluded thorough engagement on the potential utilisation of the security sector in response to the pandemic. Concerns around the lack of thorough debate was summarised by the Public Administration and Constitutional Affairs Committee, following an inquiry to scrutinise the constitutional and public administration aspects of the Coronavirus Act. A report published in December 2020 states,

> The current system of Parliamentary scrutiny in relation to lockdown regulations is not satisfactory. The fact that this legislation, which contains stark restrictions on people's civil liberties, is not amendable by Members, made under the urgent procedure and therefore without parliamentary scrutiny or effective oversight, coupled with the extremely quick passing of the Coronavirus Act means the framework Parliamentary scrutiny of the government's handling of COVID-19 is inadequate (House of Commons 2020).

Despite the lack of scrutiny through debate during the initial lockdown period, transparency improved as Parliament took up its regular programme through hybrid plenary and committee sittings. Between March 2020 and March 2021, there were many plenary sessions related to Covid-19, of which five focussed specifically on defence in relation to Covid-19 (House of Commons) and two focussed on Covid-19 and policing (in both Houses). On 21 January 2021, the House of Commons held a comprehensive debate on the defence support in the national Covid-19 response, which was titled Covid-19: Defence Support.

Committee-level debate around the security sector showed improvement over 2020. There are several committees tasked to oversee the security sector, most of which are open to the public (excluding the Intelligence and Security Committee of Parliament). The Defence Committee that oversees the expenditure, administration and policy of the Ministry of Defence continued its regular meetings immediately after the Easter recess, focusing on 14 inquiries before it. One inquiry focused specifically on the defence contribution to the UK's pandemic response (November 2020). The Home Affairs Committee oversees the work of the Home Office that includes the policing function. The Committee opened an inquiry on 11 March 2020 on the Home Office's preparedness for Covid-19. Part of the inquiry focussed on the impact of Covid-19 on wider policing, such as challenges faced in policing during lockdown, differences in approach taken by different police forces to enforce the lockdown rules, deployment and combating domestic abuse during a lockdown. Additionally, the inquiry considered 'the quality of support provided to frontline police staff, both in carrying out their duties and in coping with the increased demands placed on them' (Home Affairs Committee 2020).

The debates of the security sector committees are also closely aligned to Parliament's use of *special inquiries*. During 2020/21, Parliament initiated 57 special inquiries focussed on Covid-19, of which 51 were in the House of Commons and six in the House of Lords. As noted, both the Defence and Home Affairs committees held special inquiries into the role of the security sector during Covid-19. Despite the in-depth inquiries by primary committees, no subcommittees were specifically tasked with in-depth inquiry into the security sector and Covid-19. The Defence

Committee established a defence sub-committee which undertook three specific inquiries, related to the security of 5G, foreign involvement in the defence supply chain and women in the armed forces. While the focus of these subcommittees does not specifically lie with the military's role during the pandemic, it does demonstrate an ongoing willingness to utilise this tool, arguably leaving room for the primary Defence Committee to continue its work on the inquiry related to defence during the pandemic. Furthermore, as was the case in other countries, the use of oversight visits to gain evidence and boost transparency of the security sector was hampered by the pandemic. For example, the Defence Committee planned several oversight visits for 2020, including domestic and international locations, related to the Integrated Security, Defence and Foreign Policy Review project. Although not clearly stated, it is safe to assume that the visits did not take place due to severe travel restrictions. The Home Affairs Committee conducted several overseas visits during 2019, but none were scheduled for 2020.

In conjunction with debates, *parliamentary questions* were a prominent oversight tool used during the Covid-19 lockdown. From March 2020 to March 2021, MPs used written parliamentary questions extensively with a total of 469 questions specifically related to Covid-19. Of the total written questions, 257 were asked to the Ministry of Defence, of which 211 were from the House of Commons and 46 from the House of Lords. Similarly, during this period, 212 written questions related to Covid-19 and policing were posed to the Home Office, of which 156 questions were from the House of Commons and 55 questions from the House of Lords.

The only oversight tool not utilised thoroughly in terms of security sector oversight during the pandemic relates to the use of *external audit*. The National Audit Office (NAO) concluded two external audits on defence in 2020, but these related to the Ministry of Defence's Equipment Plan and the delivery of defence capabilities from the acquisition process (NAO 2020a). The last NAO report on the police was published in 2018 on the financial sustainability of police forces in England and Wales. While the possibility of future audits on the security sector's expenditure and roles during Covid-19 cannot be excluded, there are currently no indications of such a requirement.

In terms of the *transparency of parliament* itself, the UK Parliament fosters high-level openness of its oversight of the security sector through their digital platforms, including live streams, websites and social media. The UK Parliament website is user-friendly and contains all relevant parliamentary information on the security sector, including written and oral questions, Hansard, committee reports and minutes, and written evidence and transcript of oral evidence in committees.

Security sector accountability during Covid-19

South Africa

While the utilisation of oversight tools in the South African Parliament improved during 2020, the impact thereof on accountability of the security sector requires the correct focus areas to be covered. Amid broad sector utilisation in the initial phases of the Covid-19 pandemic, accountability depended on Parliament's oversight of deployments. Section 201(3) of the 1996 Constitution of the Republic of South Africa states that, should the Defence Force be employed, the President must inform Parliament of: (a) the reasons for the employment; (b) any place where the force is being employed; (c) the number of people involved; and (d) the period of employment. While the initial deployment of the SANDF commenced on 26 March 2020, Parliament's Joint Standing Committee on Defence only met on 22 April 2020 to consider the President's deployment letters. Similarly, the Portfolio Committee on Police only met on 29 April 2020 on the police's lockdown management. This delay in oversight of one of the largest security sector deployments in post-1994 democratic South Africa undermined the principles of good SSG, as it limited opportunities for participatory decision-making and did not involve Parliament in setting clear expectations for the security sector. It can therefore be considered a clear example of executive overreach, not due to executive action, but parliamentary inaction.

As part of accountability for the deployments, the SANDF was required to account for at least 23 cases of alleged misconduct by the SANDF that were reported to the Military Ombud. The Joint Standing Committee on Defence held an in-depth meeting with the Minister of Defence, SANDF and the Military Ombud on 22 April 2020 on its deployments and the status of investigations into misconduct. No specific recommendations flowed from the engagement since investigations were still ongoing (PMG 2020d). The Portfolio Committee on Police's meeting on 29 April 2020 raised a number of concerns about the utilisation of the police to regulate the lockdown. MPs raised concerns around reported police brutality, the high number of cases brought against police officers, the slow speed at which disciplinary hearings are concluded and how the police are responding to cases of gender-based violence. Despite these crucial areas of inquiry being pursued, no specific recommendations flowed from the engagement (PMG 2020b). A follow-up meeting was held on 8 May 2020 that included a briefing by the Independent Police Investigative Directorate, which was requested to provide the Committee with a list of Covid-19 deployment-related cases against police members. The matter of gender-based violence again received attention, although no in-depth inquiry was made in this regard (PMG 2020c). No formal reports on the Covid-19 deployments were tabled in the Houses of Parliament by either the defence or police committees.

While these initial committee engagements were positive in maintaining accountability, the lack of clear recommendations detract from concrete contributions to accountability. For example, when compared to the judicial branch of government, a clear distinction is visible, specifically in relation to the ruling by the High Court of South Africa (Gauteng Division) on 15 May 2020 in the case of the Khosa family against the Ministers of Defence and Police, among others. The Judge's Draft Order noted that 'the rule of separation of powers cannot be used to avoid the obligation of a court to provide appropriate relief that is just and equitable to a litigant who successfully raises a constitutional complaint' (Case Number 21512/2020, 2020). The Draft Order therefore went much further than Parliament's oversight committees in ensuring accountability by reaffirming and/or ordering, among others, the following:

- Confirming the Constitutional rights of all persons to human dignity, the right to life, the right not to be tortured or to be treated in a degrading way.
- Confirming that the security forces must instruct their members to act in accordance with the Constitution and the law.
- Members of the security forces should only use minimum force.
- Members of the security forces are bound by the Prevention and Combating of Torture Act (Act No. 13 of 2013) and relevant UN conventions.
- The SANDF must, pending disciplinary action, put on precautionary leave all members present during the death of Mr Khosa.
- All security forces must develop and publish a Code of Conduct and operational procedures relating to its deployment during the State of Disaster.
- The security sector must establish a freely accessible mechanism for civilians to report allegations of cruel or inhumane treatment.
- Ensure investigations into the alleged incidents are completed and reports submitted to the Court within three weeks.

While the judgment should be viewed as highly critical of the executive's control of the security sector, it indirectly raises questions around Parliament's oversight role. The Order's focus on the use of minimum force and compliance with the law are areas that fall within the ambit of parliamentary oversight. It also links oversight of the security sector's training and education to ensure fit-for-purpose forces. Parliament's defence committees did consider evidence in this regard during Covid-19 deployments, albeit to a limited extent. The Joint Standing Committee on Defence was informed that 'further training interventions would be conducted for members of the SANDF who were deployed in order to address any gaps necessary to improve the conduct of the members' (PMG 2020d). Subsequently, the committees were informed that the DOD was utilising training courses to ensure a culture of ethics and accountability (PMG 2020a). While training matters were addressed by the defence committees, it did so in passing and not in-depth. The Portfolio Committee on Police was more successful in this regard. MPs posed specific questions on how training would address alleged brutality during the Covid-19 deployments. The Minister of Police provided specific responses on training to enhance ethical behaviour and how this training is conducted through workshops (PMG 2020c). Further, the judgment's focus on the need for a dedicated Code of Conduct for the Covid-19 deployments highlights the need for parliamentary oversight of policy and legislative guidelines. For example, Section 19(3)(c)(i) of the Defence Act (42 of 2002) states that when the SANDF is deployed with the police, such duties 'must be performed in accordance with a code of conduct and operational procedures approved by the Minister'. This requirement was not considered by the defence or police committees.

Parliament's oversight of the security sector's Covid-19-related budget and procurement processes showed continuity when committees resumed their activities. Discussions around Covid-19 related expenditure formed part of most defence and police committee meetings, as there was overlap between annual budgetary planning and the ongoing Covid-19 expenditure. Both the Portfolio Committees on Police as well as Defence and Military Veterans considered the Government's Special Adjustments Budget on 15 June 2020 that made specific provision for Covid-19. Budgetary shifts also formed part of discussions around the departmental annual reports and quarterly consideration of departmental expenditure. Oversight of procurement in the defence realm revolved largely around the work of the Auditor-General and the special report on irregular Covid-19 expenditure in the Department. Two parliamentary engagements held in February 2021 did not result in substantial recommendations, but allowed for departmental and other investigations to continue, with future parliamentary oversight considered. The Portfolio Committee on Police held a meeting on 10 July 2020 wherein MPs questioned discrepancies in PPE costs and requested a complete breakdown of prices (PMG 2020e). By March 2021, oversight of procurement irregularities was ongoing at the defence and police committees.

Finally, the police and defence committees did exercise oversight over aspects related to human resources and equipment. The former related largely to ongoing inquiry, both at committee level and through parliamentary questions, on the number of SANDF personnel deployed. Oversight of the latter focused on the availability of PPE for both military and defence personnel deployed. For example, the Portfolio Committee on Police's engagement with the police on 10 July 2020 included an overview of employee health and wellness and logistical matters (PMG 2020e). Of concern, however, is the gap in oversight during the initial Covid-19 outbreak and subsequent lockdown. A clear need existed for oversight to ensure sufficient PPE availability to security sector personnel that were considered to be rendering essential services.

The Philippines

From the previous section, it is evident that the Philippines Parliament utilised some of the tools at its disposal to conduct oversight. It was further evident that there were severe limitations on oversight of the security sector, specifically during the initial phases of the Covid-19 pandemic, while a lack of adequate committee minutes complicates an investigation into the true nature of security sector oversight. When reviewing the specific focus areas for security sector oversight, it becomes apparent that Parliament did not conduct in-depth oversight over a number of these areas. Parliamentary records do not reveal thorough oversight of, for example, security sector deployments, despite the military being utilised in a supporting role with the PNP and the extended role of the PNP in enforcing the lockdown. What is evident though is a reactionary oversight capacity after Parliament reconvened. While the deployment itself was not overseen, a parliamentary inquiry into cases of misconduct by security forces was launched through the Committee on Human Rights, as noted in the previous section.

Oversight of policy and legislative guidelines related to the utilisation of the security sector during Covid-19 was also absent, as is evident from the limited discussions on security matters during the consideration of the Bayanihan 1 and Bayanihan 2. Parliament's National Defense and Security Committee did not return to matters of deployment-related policy after committee activity recommenced, but continued to focus on broader policy oversight. For example, on 13 November 2020, the National Defense and Security Committee's Technical Working Group approved the draft bill to establish a Philippine Self-Reliant Defense Posture Program and a national defence industry. The bill repeals legislation authorising the Secretary of National Defense to enter into defence contracts to implement projects under the self-reliant defence programmes, and appropriating funds thereof (Committee Affairs Department 2020c). Notably, on 10 March 2020, just prior to the national lockdown, the Standing Committee on Public Order and Safety discussed legislation to provide the necessary support for the modernisation of the facilities and equipment of the PNP with the goal of improving its readiness and capacity to respond to peace and order problems (Committee Affairs Department 2020d). This provided a clear platform to ensure PNP readiness during the Covid-19 pandemic which remain unused as Parliament resumed normal oversight activities. Matters related to security sector human resources and equipment were also not considered during the immediate aftermath of lockdown enforcement, despite surfacing serious allegations of abuse of power and human rights violations. As the Covid-19 response was deemed highly militarised by the UN, it could have benefitted from an effective parliamentary counterweight to ensure accountability.

Rather than in-depth inquiry around the roles, functions and utilisation of the security sector during Covid-19, it seems as if Parliament chose to continue with its standard agenda of security sector oversight. This is evident in, for example, committee debates just prior to the initial lockdown period and towards the end of 2020. The Standing Committee on Public Order and Safety held debates on the revitalisation of the national police (10 March 2020), the Subcommittee on Police Administration (Public Order and Safety) repealed legislation on height requirements for applicants to the police (and other safety structures) (27 November 2020) and the Standing Committee on National Defense and Security debated (13 November 2020) on improving the defence posture. These meetings indicate that there were attempts to oversee the security sector and advance accountability and a return to normal oversight activities of the security sector towards the end of 2020, albeit at the exclusion of thorough Covid-19 related deployment oversight.

Oversight of Covid-19 budgetary and procurement related aspects showed limited depth, specifically in relation to security sector expenditure. First, it was already noted that matters related to procurement received attention through Senate Resolution (No. 479, 2020) that called on the COA to conduct a special audit on Covid-19 related spending, loans and donations under the Bayanihan 1. Although this provision came well after reported procurement irregularities, it nonetheless reflects ongoing oversight. The level of accountability to be achieved will depend on Parliament's insistence to include security sector procurement and the subsequent oversight thereof. Second, in terms of budgetary oversight, the Philippine Congress, through the approval of the Bayanihan Heals as One Act, 2020, empowered the President to redirect state funds for the immediate response to the Covid-19 pandemic. According to the Congressional Policy and Budget Research Department (CPBRD), the four major provisions of Regulation 11469 grant important budgetary powers to the President:

• Explore how the Ministry of Defence has ensured that potential adversaries have not taken advantage of the need to focus on the pandemic response.

As Parliament resumed normal oversight activities after the initial lockdown, its high volume of activities reflected elevated levels of oversight of most key focus areas for the security sector. The comprehensive House of Commons plenary on the armed forces' Covid-19 support held on 21 January 2021 addressed a variety of issues, including human resources and equipment. Specific discussions were held on the health and welfare of soldiers in terms of regular testing and vaccinations. Further focus fell on the continued deployment of the armed forces and specifically in terms of the vaccination rollout, the continuation of NATO operations, and maintenance of crucial defence tasks (Hansard UK Parliament 2021). During oral questions in the House of Commons, the Secretary of State for the Home Department assured Members that the police were given guidance and funding to support them in dealing with Covid-19, and confirmed that 20,000 police officers will be recruited. Coupled hereto is the Defence Committee's inquiry into defence contributions to the UK's pandemic response that is posed to achieve a high level of accountability and lead to concrete recommendations and possible reform.

Debates, both at plenary and committee level, written and oral questions and special inquiries covered the most important focus areas of oversight. In terms of the security sector's budgetary and procurement oversight for expenditure during Covid-19, the Defence Committee examined the Ministry of Defence Annual Report and Accounts 2019/20 on 08 December 2020. The meeting focused on expenditure and the effects of Covid-19 on the recruitment and the initial training in the armed forces. The funding of defence formed part of the discussions on the inquiry into defence's contribution to the UK's pandemic response (24 November 2020).

Both the Defence Committee and Defence Subcommittee addressed security sector issues related to health and wellbeing, and gender and ethic inclusivity that are often neglected in parliamentary oversight. The Defence Committee examined the mental health support provided to the armed forces and veterans, and whether the Covid-19 pandemic led to additional challenges in mental health. The Defence Subcommittee established an inquiry into the experience of female service personnel, challenges faced and whether current policies are addressing these challenges (Defence Subcommittee 2020). While not specifically tasked to review these aspects in relation to Covid-19 deployments, the continuation of the inquiry during this period is relevant. The challenges that the inquiry addressed included, inter alia, the recruitment and retention of female personnel; incidences of sexual offences; bullying and harassment complaints; and, transition to civilian life where female service leavers have lower employment rates (Defence Subcommittee 2020).

In March 2020, the Home Affairs Committee held a non-inquiry session with evidence on police ethnic diversity and institutional racism. The session was relevant to the historic Macpherson Inquiry and Report (1997), which investigated the racially motivated death of Stephen Lawrence on 22 April 1993. The Report concluded that the investigation into the killing had been 'marred by a combination of professional incompetence, institutional racism and a failure of leadership' and made 70 recommendations relating to racism (Quinn 2019). A key outcome of the Report was the establishment of the Independent Police Complaints Commission to investigate police misconduct and criminality. This session formed part of the Home Affairs Committee Inquiry titled, 'The Macpherson Report: Twenty-one years on'. In addition to new evidence on police and race, the inquiry included concerns raised about the policing of the Covid-19 lockdown and reported disproportionality of fines and investigations of individuals from black and minority ethnic communities (Home Affairs Committee 2020b). Further, the Home Affairs Committee established an inquiry into police conduct and complaints in August 2020 to examine the role of the Independent Office for Police Conduct in relation to the police conduct and discipline system and, examine possible reforms to secure public confidence in the police conduct and disciplinary system (Home Affairs Committee 2020a).

Linking Covid-19 responses and SDG16

This chapter provided an account of the utilisation of the security sector during the first year of the Covid-19 pandemic, as well as parliamentary responses thereto in South Africa, the Philippines and the UK. These responses, be it by the executive arm of government or parliament, provides a snapshot of both the contributions and detractions that the security sector and parliament can make to SDG16.

In terms of the utilisation of the security sector, the case studies reveal both the extreme positive and negative impact of the sector on the SDGs. Although not the primary focus of this study, the utilisation of the security sector in South Africa, the Philippines and the UK contributed to SDG3C: 'Strengthen the capacity of all countries, in particular developing countries, for early warning, risk reduction and management of national and global health risks' (United Nations, 2016). This was primarily achieved through military humanitarian assistance, the transport of PPE, medical equipment, testing kits and frontline personnel. The security sector, notably the military in South Africa and the Philippines, and the police in all three countries, further aided the pandemic response through the enforcement of national lockdowns to prevent disease spread, which also contributed to maintaining the rule of law (SDG16.3). This securitised approach did, however, also detract from SDG16. In South Africa and the Philippines, several deaths at the hands of the security sector were recorded, affecting the attainment of SDG16.1 that focuses on the reduction of violence and deaths. The very institutions that ought to reduce violence and related deaths caused such instances, which also detracted from SDG16.3 (maintaining the rule of law). The utilisation of the security sector for the maintenance of domestic peace and security requires a careful balancing against SDG16A which calls for the strengthening of national institutions to prevent violence and combat crime. The Covid-19 case studies reveal that strengthening the security sector, including the strengthening of legislation for its utilisation, should be balanced and cognisant of the sector's potential to detract from SDG16.

The parliaments of South Africa, the Philippines and the UK showed varying SSG capacity during Covid-19, specifically during the initial period of the pandemic. During this period, none of the parliaments in the three countries studied were fully functional. In both South Africa and the UK, lockdown restrictions were enforced through regulations not subject to parliamentary scrutiny. Similarly, in the Philippines, Parliament ceded significant power to the executive. In addition to the political concerns this poses in terms of a system of checks and balances as per the trias politica, it affects the achievement of several SDG16 targets. SDG16.3 aims at ensuring the rule of law and equal access to justice for all and parliaments, through their legislative and oversight functions, present a means of ensuring justice for all. Where secondary legislation is used to bypass parliament, it undermines the checks put in place to ensure justice. The inactivity of parliaments in the three countries during the initial outbreak of the pandemic further detracted from SDG16.7, aiming to ensure participatory and representative decision-making, specifically given parliaments' key representation function.

The inactivity of the three parliaments during the initial pandemic outbreak affected the achievement of SDG16.6, aimed at developing effective, accountable and transparent institutions. Parliaments exercised no or limited oversight of the security sector utilisation during this period, negatively affecting accountability of the sector. This is particularly relevant in South Africa and the Philippines where parliaments failed to hold the security sector to immediate account as instances of power abuses emerged. However, the positive role that parliaments can play in terms of SDG16.6 became apparent as parliaments resumed their functions. The South African parliamentary defence committees called to account the Minister of Defence, SANDF and Military Ombud for power abuses by soldiers. The UK Defence Committee also launched an inquiry into the defence contribution to the UK's pandemic response. The resumption of normal oversight and budgeting functions of defence and police committees in the three countries, in the context of the Covid-19 pandemic, contributed to SDG16. Security sector human resources and equipment oversight were reviewed in South Africa and the UK. Oversight of these aspects contributed to the security sector's ability to respond to the pandemic and fulfil its required security functions, thus adding to SDG16A (the strengthening of national institutions).

SDG16.6 also calls for transparency and the initial inactivity of the three parliaments severely detracted from attaining this target. Parliaments are important institutions for the collation and dissemination of information on the security sector and the lack of debate due to institutional inactivity prevented this crucial function. The inactivity also detracted from SDG16.10 aimed at ensuring public access to information. Nonetheless, the recovery in functioning restored the parliaments' contribution to SDG16.6 and SDG16.10 when committee debates resumed in all three countries studied, adding to transparency around security sector activity during Covid-19. Of particular importance was the use of external audit as an oversight tool by the South African and Philippines parliaments to oversee procurement irregularities during the pandemic, including in the security sector. Such inquiries demonstrate the value of the oversight tool in addressing SDG16.5: 'Substantially reduce corruption and bribery in all their forms' (United Nations 2016). The South African and Philippines case studies reveal concerns in terms of the accessibility of parliamentary information around the security sector. These concerns pre-date the Covid-19 pandemic, but the pandemic arguably illuminated this shortcoming and provides an area in need for attention to realise both parliament's full contribution to SDG16.6 and SDG16.10.

Conclusion

The security sector was used in different capacities around the world and the South African, Philippines and UK case studies reflect this diversity. The case studies also reflect diverse outcomes in the utilisation of the security sector. The sector's positive contribution to human security was on display in the three countries through its humanitarian aid. However, the sector also detracted from human security in a number of ways, ranging from a reported growth in distrust between the police and community to the death of citizens. Of specific importance is that during the initial Covid-19 pandemic outbreak, parliaments in all three case studies failed to rise to the occasion to ensure thorough, continued and in-depth accountability and transparency. With parliaments going into recess, less information on security sector activity was forthcoming, hampering information flows and transparency of the sector. Parliaments also rushed through legislation or allowed the extended use of secondary legislation that invariably gave rise to executive dominance, undermining the very principle of a system of checks and balances as envisaged under the trias politica. This disruption of the balance in power and a rise in executive dominance comes with elevated risk where the large scale domestic security sector deployments occur, specifically when such deployments are not specifically limited to humanitarian aid. Although the private security sector service was deemed essential in all three countries, even specifically noted as a force multiplier in the Philippines, little information was available and there was no evidence of parliamentary scrutiny.

Parliament's oversight resolve returned once parliamentary activities resumed after lockdown, as is evident in the three case studies. Oversight of ongoing security sector deployments did, however, vary significantly between countries. The UK Parliament launched several in-depth inquiries related to the security sector's utilisation. In South Africa, security sector utilisation formed part of standard ongoing oversight activities, notably committee meetings. In the Philippines, oversight of the security sector's utilisation during Covid-19 was, however, limited and a return to normal parliamentary activity did not result in in-depth inquiry. In both South Africa and the Philippines, where serious human rights abuses occurred, parliamentary oversight made a concerted effort to address these cases. However, shortcomings are immediately noticeable in the slow progression in this regard, as well as parliaments allowing the executive to drive the investigative side of the inquiry. The case studies therefore demonstrate a need for a more rapid parliamentary reaction capability, especially in cases of extraordinary utilisation of the security forces. Where parliaments lack this capacity and where executive dominance is allowed to manifest, it undermines the principles of accountability and transparency sought in SDG16.6 and SDG16.10. Where human security is at risk due to the extraordinary utilisation of the security forces, a lack of accountability and transparency can further detract from SDG16 in its entirety.

CHAPTER 5

Conclusion and Recommendations to Parliaments

Introduction

This study drew together a number of aspects related to the concept of good governance and its interrelation with the SDGs, notably SDG16. Viewing the targets encapsulated in SDG16 as desired outcomes, the study utilised the principles of good SSG as a foundation and reviewed the contributions of the security sector and parliaments to these outcomes. The study was based on two assumptions confirmed by existing literature considered during the research. First, a professional security sector can contribute to the achievement of peace, security and stability, which is a prerequisite for sustainable development. Second, the security sector contributes to peace and stability through accountability. For these contributions to manifest, the security sector requires effective systems of governance and checks and balances. Parliaments form an integral part of the system of checks and balances in democratic governance structures and therefore the link between parliaments, the security sector and good SSG, as enablers of SDG16, were reviewed. The review was carried over to the three selected case studies that analysed the utilisation of the security sector in response to Covid-19 between March 2020 and March 2021, as well as the parliamentary response. This chapter provides the main conclusions of the research and draws on the case studies to propose key recommendations for parliaments in their contribution to the achievement of SDG16.

Conclusions

Confirming the security sector contribution to SDG16

SDG16 aims to promote just, peaceful and inclusive societies and set 12 targets for achievement by 2030. This study drew on existing research to demonstrate that the security sector can be a

---

How to cite this book chapter:
Janse van Rensburg, W., van Zyl-Gous, N., and Heinecken, L. 2022. *Parliaments' Contributions to Security Sector Governance/Reform and the Sustainable Development Goals: Testing Parliaments' Resolve in Security Sector Governance During Covid-19.* Pp. 61–67. London: Ubiquity Press. DOI: https://doi.org /10.5334/bcr.e. License: CC-BY-NC

valuable contributor to a number of the targets set under SDG16. The military contributes to peace and security through its traditional 'war-making' role, which has gained specific value in the form of peacekeeping and peace enforcement operations. Through the responsible use of militaries in their traditional roles, militaries can contribute to the reduction of violence and deaths (SDG16.1), reduction in abuse, exploitation, trafficking (SDG16.2), promotion of the rule of law (SDG16.3) and the reduction of illicit financial and arms flows (SDG16.4). Militaries are also increasingly contributing to stability in non-traditional or humanitarian roles. Police forces' contributions to SDG16's targets are even more pronounced in that they maintain the rule of law (SDG16.3 and SDG16B) within states, a key component for the establishment of just societies. The private security sector is increasingly drawn into policing functions, be it through collaboration, or the outsourcing of security tasks. These examples show the potential positive contribution of the sector to the ideals postulated in SDG16. To a large extent, the research confirmed these contributions through consulting existing literature, but further reviewed this in the three Covid-19 case studies.

Covid-19 presented most states with a major non-military humanitarian threat that impacted directly on human security, a core underlying theme of SDG16. In many countries, the security sector became a key role-player in the state's responses to the pandemic. The utilisation of the security sector varied, but its positive contributions in terms of humanitarian aid in many states is evident. This was reflected in the case studies where the militaries of South Africa, the Philippines and the UK were utilised to, for example, transport medical equipment and provide assistance to local healthcare facilities. Such aid highlights the positive impact that the military can have when utilised in a non-traditional role not only in terms of SDG16, but several other SDGs such as SDG3 promoting good health and wellbeing, as well as SDG6, promoting clean water and sanitation. The use of police services to restrict movement to prevent the spread of Covid-19 provides a further example of positive humanitarian contributions by the security sector. The case studies therefore confirm existing literature on the potential for positive contributions to various SDGs by the security sector.

The case studies did, however, reveal that the utilisation of the security sector has the potential to detract from SDG16. In many states, the Covid-19 pandemic brought about the utilisation of military personnel in a law enforcement capacity in addition to its humanitarian role. In both South Africa and the Philippines, these deployments resulted in severe cases of brutality by the military and police, even resulting in the loss of life, thus detracting from SDG16.1. These incidents reflect the potential negative impact of security sector utilisation outside a humanitarian support role and the devastating effect this can have on efforts to maintain human security. What this illustrates is that where the military is involved in internal roles, oversight is necessary to ensure that soldiers are properly trained, funded and prepared for these missions. In addition, one should be alert to the potential impact that the securitisation of health issues, and other disasters, may have on the militarisation of society, where military rather than developmental approaches are used as a form of response. Concerns around securitisation links to another requirement highlighted by SDG16.6, namely the need for accountable and transparent institutions, including the security sector.

Confirming parliaments' shortfalls in emergencies

While many institutions aid the transparency and accountability of the security sector, parliaments are important institutions for accountability. Parliaments may well not be the panacea in addressing issues related to security sector accountability but, through its legislative, representation and oversight functions, it can aid in the security sector's positive contribution to SDG16 outcomes. Similarly, parliaments can use their mandate to limit opportunities for the security sector to detract from SDG16. The power of parliaments in directing the security sector's positive contribution to SDG16 lies in the various functions they fulfil. The study primarily highlighted parliaments' budgetary function as well as the use of key internationally accepted oversight tools, including parliamentary debates, questions, oversight visits, ad hoc committees and external audit capacity. The study further drew on existing literature to identify the key areas for oversight that enable parliaments to effectively oversee the security sector. The centrality of committees as the engine-rooms of parliaments and as key enablers of security sector oversight were emphasised. Despite rich existing literature on parliamentary oversight of the security sector, and thoroughly entrenched global oversight practices, the Covid-19 pandemic brought before parliaments a unique set of challenges that threatened the quality of its impact on the security sector.

The impact of Covid-19 on parliaments was immediately evident with the global spread of the pandemic and posed a real threat to democratic systems of checks and balances and good govern-ance. The case studies reveal that the South African, Philippines and UK parliaments were initially ill equipped to perform their functions outside the confines of physical legislatures. This is of particular importance to oversight of the security sector as parliamentary inactivity in the imme-diate lockdown periods overlapped with the unprecedented deployment of security forces. Lim-ited opportunity for oversight and budgetary monitoring of these massive deployments were thus initially available. The limited parliamentary activity during this period is even more concerning given the threat of executive overreach. In South Africa, the executive used secondary legislation (regulations) to enforce the lockdown restrictions, without parliamentary input or scrutiny. In the Philippines, Parliament approved emergency legislation quickly without following normal proce-dures, providing significant power to the executive branch of government. In the UK, Parliament too approved emergency legislation quickly, forgoing normal processes to enable the Govern-ment's response, but the executive promulgated the secondary legislation that enforced the lock-down restriction, without any parliamentary input or scrutiny. The research therefore suggests that this lull in parliamentary oversight gave rise to executive dominance and limited oversight of the security sector. While not the case in all countries, this initial oversight void created a vacuum within which the likelihood of security sector misconduct is elevated, potentially detracting from SDG16's main aim of just and peaceful societies.

Highlighting the link between continuous oversight, accountability and the SDGs

The study further highlights that despite the initial lull in parliamentary activity, the UK, South African and Philippines parliaments showed remarkable adaptability. The value of this observa-tion lies in the subsequent oversight of the security sector that followed as parliaments adopted remote working methods and committee activities resumed. In the three countries reviewed, this allowed for a return to relatively normal oversight, budgetary, representation and legislative func-tioning. Of specific focus was parliaments' budgetary function related to the security sector that gained traction in South Africa and the UK, specifically the consideration of adjusted budgets for Covid-19. The normalisation of oversight also allowed the South African and Philippines parlia-ments to delve deeper into procurement irregularities, specifically through the use of external audit functions. The improvement in oversight demonstrates the need for continuity in the over-sight process to ensure elevated levels of accountability in order to achieve SDG16.6, as well as linkages with other SDG16 targets aimed at reducing corruption (SDG16.5) and improving access to information (SDG16.10).

The amount of information that flows from continuous parliamentary oversight assists in driv-ing the levels of transparency around the security sector. The study reflected on how parliamentary oversight activities contribute to a sector that is often shrouded in secrecy. A lack of transparency of the sector as a result of limited parliamentary activity in South Africa, the Philippines and the UK were evident during the initial lockdown periods. As oversight improved, significantly more information was forthcoming on aspects related to expenditure, procurement, deployment, misconduct, etc. The study confirms the link between parliamentary oversight and security sector transparency. The study also found that the adoption of virtual platforms for oversight did, in some cases, add to transparency of both the security sector and parliaments itself. Nonetheless, some concerns around parliamentary transparency that pre-dated Covid-19 became amplified during this period. The South African and Philippines case studies highlight concerns around the lack of easily accessible, structured and searchable information on parliamentary activities around the security sector. Limited transparency of both parliament and the security sector detracts directly from SDG16.6 which demands accountability and transparency of institutions at *all* levels as well as SDG16.10 requiring public access to information.

Human security theory and the concept of executive dominance

Although not the main aim of the study, the research reveals concerns around executive dominance in emergency situations, as during the Covid-19 pandemic, and the potential impact thereof on the achievement of the SDGs. The UN noted a heavily militarised lockdown culture in many countries across the world. The rush to utilise the security sector as a main actor in state response, coupled with executive dominance, raises significant concern around the potential impact on SSG in a democratic context. In many states, security forces were used, under the guise of humanitarian efforts to combat Covid-19, to suppress political opposition. Freedom House research indicates that 'since the coronavirus outbreak began, the condition of democracy and human rights has grown worse in 80 countries' (Repucci & Slipowitz 2020). The use of security forces during Covid-19 brings into question, at least in some states, the aim of the sector as a contributor or enabler of human security. Rather, it shows that when the conditions allow, security institutions can be misappropriated as agents of state- or even regime security. At a theoretic level, these concerns around the securitisation of non-conventional security issues highlight the need for further SSG studies as viewed through an expanded theory of security outside the confines of human security.

Recommendations to parliaments

DCAF postulates that parliaments fulfil five primary functions, including legislative, budgetary, oversight, elective and representation functions. Within the scope of the Covid-19 case study, all functions except the elective function reflected the potential to either amplify or diminish the contributions of security sector to SDG16. The recommendations below highlight means through which parliaments can aid the security sector to elevate its SDG16 contributions.

Parliaments' legislative function

Checks and balances for domestic deployments of the military. The case studies, with specific reference to the cases of misconduct in South Africa and the Philippines, highlight the risks associated with deploying the military in a domestic policing capacity. These risks can detract considerably from SDG16.3 calling for the promotion of the rule of law, as well as SDG16.1 which is aimed at the reduction of violence. Deployments with this mandate have an invariably higher risk than purely humanitarian domestic deployments, as is evident from the UK's utilisation of its military during Covid-19. This risk of putting the military in direct policing contact with the citizenry through law enforcement and order functions also has the potential to cause lasting damage to the state of civil-military relations. However, from time to time it may be necessary for states to amplify its policing capacity by using the military, but then these roles should be clearly defined and the military properly trained, funded and structured for such roles. *Parliaments should ensure*

1. To direct the discontinuance of appropriated programmes, projects or activities of any agency of the Executive Department including government-owned or controlled corporations in the financial years 2019 and 2020 General Appropriations Act whether released or unreleased, but the allotments for which remain unobligated; the savings from which will be used to augment identified priorities [Section 4 (v)].
2. To authorise that any unutilised or unreleased balance in a special purpose fund, as of the date of declaration of the State of Emergency, shall be considered to have their purpose abandoned for the duration of the State of Emergency [Section 4 (w)].
3. To reprogramme, reallocate and realign from savings on other items of appropriations in the financial year 2020 General Appropriations Act; and that all amounts so reprogrammed, reallocated or realigned in the Executive Department shall be deemed automatically appropriated for measures to address the COVID-19 situation [Section 4 (x)].
4. To allocate cash, funds, investments, including unutilised or unreleased subsidies and transfers held by any government-owned or controlled corporations or National Government Agencies for COVID-19 emergency [Section 4 (y)] (CPBRD 2020).

Through the emergency legislation, Congress effectively released the power of the purse. Although the President reported to Congress weekly during the three months that the Bayanihan 1 Act was in full force, the reports lacked crucial information (Punongbayan 2020), especially on the security sector. The Act expired on 05 June 2020 and was succeeded by the Bayanihan 2 Act, which extended the President's powers for six months. Despite the increased utilisation of the security sector during Covid-19, Congress did not effectively hold the executive to account in terms of security sector expenditure and it thus detracted from accountability.

Ordinarily, parliamentary oversight of all budgets, including that of the security sector, is undertaken by the Appropriations Committee of the House of Representatives and the Finance Committee of the Senate and finally by the plenary of both chambers. These Committees consider 'All matters directly and principally relating to the expenditures of the national government including the payment of public indebtedness, creation, abolition and classification of positions in government, and the determination of salaries, allowances and benefits of government personnel' (Aguja n.d.). The Appropriations Committee deliberated on the proposed 2021 budget and previous years' performance of the Department of Defense on 08 September 2020 (Committee Affairs Department 2020a) and on that of the Department of Interior and Local Government (DILG) budget on 10 September 2020, of which the PNP is an agency (Committee Affairs Department 2020b). These engagements again reflect a return to normal budgetary oversight of the security sector towards the end of 2020, albeit with limited specific focus on expenditure of the security sector's utilisation during the pandemic.

The United Kingdom

The utilisation of oversight tools in the UK Parliament remained at a high standard despite an initial decrease during lockdown periods. However, these periods had an arguably limited impact on accountability of the security sector because of the array of oversight focus areas covered during 2020/21. Of particular relevance to accountability is the Defence Committee's inquiry into defence deployments by reviewing the contribution to the UK's pandemic response (November 2020). The Committee inquiry set out to:

- Assess the Ministry of Defence's planning and preparedness for a pandemic.
- Understand how the armed forces have supported civilian authority during the pandemic.
- Evaluate the effectiveness of the specific actions and activities undertaken by military and civilian personnel.

that the legislation guiding military deployments, be it domestically or internationally, are clearly defined in law. Furthermore, the role of parliament itself in relation to decisions on and oversight of deployments should be defined in law. Parliaments should ensure that there are additional checks and balances, through legislation, to reduce the risks associated with the domestic deployments of the military in a policing capacity. This may include a broader scope for ex ante parliamentary approval of domestic deployments and improved oversight and accountability criteria.

Addressing the use of secondary legislation as a means of circumventing parliamentary oversight. By intention or not, the South African and UK case studies reveal how the use of secondary legislation, or regulations, can be used in emergencies to circumvent effective parliamentary oversight. This has the potential to give rise to executive dominance, including the use of the security sector. Executive dominance is not only in conflict with the democratic ideals of checks and balances, but also with SDG16.6 calling for accountable and transparent institutions. Parliamentary oversight is required to continuously oversee the sector to ensure, among others, that it contributes to SDG16 outcomes. *Legislation should limit the prolonged use of secondary legislation that restricts basic human rights and parliamentary oversight, specifically when the security sector is deployed by the executive.*

Formally aligning security sector utilisation with the SDGs. The Philippines Parliament, through the Bayanihan Heal as One Act, provided the executive with significant powers to respond to the pandemic, including in its utilisation of the security sector. Although weekly feedback from the executive was received, the Act lacked clarity on the specifics of the security forces' utilisation to be provided to Parliament. The military has the potential to contribute to the SDGs and while the executive is responsible for its utilisation, it remains accountable to parliament. *Parliaments should enact legislation that compels the executive to report to parliament on the reasons for, costs and expected duration of military deployments. Similar legislation can be considered for the police forces and cases of private security sector collaboration or outsourcing.*

Parliaments' representation function

Maintaining parliaments' functionality. For parliaments to effectively fulfil their representation function, ongoing oversight, budgetary monitoring and legislating is required to ensure that the will of the people is reflected in government decisions. The representation function aligns with SDG16.7 aimed at inclusive, participatory and representative decision-making. For parliaments to contribute to the achievement of SDG16, continued parliamentary activity is a prerequisite. The case studies revealed how, in most parliaments, Covid-19 caused a major break in parliamentary activity during the initial lockdown periods. Positively, the adoption of virtual practices enabled parliaments to resume their representation function. *Parliaments should maintain the alternative working methods developed during Covid-19 that allowed the institutions to remain functional outside the confines of the physical legislature. Following parliaments' return to normal functioning, the positive developments should be analysed to ensure that it could bolster existing parliamentary functioning. In terms of parliaments' oversight of the security sector, the use of virtual means allows parliaments to respond faster to security sector oversight requirements, specifically the deployment of the military. Parliaments should develop guidelines to ensure the rapid consideration of all military deployments and make use of virtual means where physical sittings are not feasible.*

Parliaments' budgetary function

Adding layers of security to prevent security sector misconduct. Cases of misconduct during the Covid-19 pandemic highlight the need for institutions that provide citizens with recourse, such as Military Ombuds institutions and independent police investigative divisions. This require-ment is important in terms of SDG16.3 calling for the rule of law, as well as SDG16B which is aimed at the promotion and enforcement of non-discriminatory laws. *Parliaments should ensure that where such institutions do not exist, the requisite legislation is considered to ensure its estab-lishment. Where Military Ombud institutions and independent police investigative divisions are in place, parliaments should use their oversight and budgetary mandates to ensure the optimal func-tioning of such institutions. This is of particular relevance during periods where the security forces are deployed in a domestic role.*

The need for continuous budgetary monitoring. The potential positive contribution by the security sector to various SDG16 targets was illuminated in the study. However, for the security sector to effectively contribute to those SDG16 targets, it requires appropriate funding to fulfil its tasks. An appropriate financial allocation is a prerequisite for SDG16A that aims at strengthening national institutions to prevent violence and combat terrorism and crime. Furthermore, where funds are allocated to the security sector, the monitoring of expenditure is essential. This not only improves accountability (SDG16.6), but also lowers the risks of corruption (SDG16.5). *Parlia-ments should ensure that the security sector is sufficiently funded to fulfil its contributions to the SDGs. Parliaments should be encouraged to consult widely on security sector funding requirements and ensure that budgeting is evidence-based. Furthermore, constant monitoring of security sector expenditure should be reflected in parliaments' oversight programmes. Parliamentary committees should ensure regular engagement with state and other external auditors to track security sector expenditure to limit the risk of corruption. Parliaments can also be encouraged to ensure consequence management is applied in cases of corruption and bribery in the security sector.*

Parliaments' oversight function

Preventing a silo-approach to security sector oversight. The security sector is a diverse sector with a multitude of role-players. Covid-19 saw the cooperative use of, for example, the military, police and other state agencies. In many states, this cooperative arrangement has been a signifi-cant challenge; yet, oversight of these cooperative deployments appear segmented in many parlia-ments. For example, in the South African Parliament, no joint meetings were held between the Portfolio Committee on Police and the Joint Standing Committee on Defence, the two primary committees in the National Assembly overseeing the deployment of the police and military. The integrated oversight approach links to the broad themes of the SDGs that often rely on multiple actors within a state for targets to be achieved. *Parliaments should ensure cooperation between the oversight structures, particularly committees, that oversee the various security sector role-players. Notably, the chairpersons of parliamentary committees should play a key role in ensuring such coop-eration, especially in instances where segments of the security sector are utilised jointly.*

Prioritising SDG16 in the context of security sector oversight. The use of the security sector during the Covid-19 pandemic and subsequent parliamentary oversight did not prioritise the SDGs. In South Africa, discussions around SDGs in oversight activities were limited or absent, notably in terms of security sector oversight. In the Philippines, which has a dedicated parlia-mentary committee looking at the achievement of the SDGs, no engagement of this committee focused on the security sector during 2020/21. There was limited tracking by parliaments of how the utilisation of the security sector during Covid-19 impacted on the attainment of the SDGs and SDG16 targets in particular. *Parliament should build capacity to track SDG16 targets, specifically in relation to oversight of the executive's use of the military and police. This is of particular relevance in the post-Covid-19 recovery phase whereby SDG16 targets could serve as a guide for parliamentary oversight. Good governance principles overlap with both parliaments' responsibilities and SDG16, and could be used as a loose framework for guiding their work building to 2030.*

Enhancing security sector transparency through parliamentary oversight. Parliaments contribute to security sector transparency through oversight activities. This is an important contribution to SDG16.10 focusing on the need for public access to information. However, the level of contribution to transparency is often hampered by the inaccessibility of parliamentary engagements with the security sector. *Parliaments must ensure easily accessible and searchable information on all its engagements with the security sector. These engagements should further be linked to SDG goals and targets and be made easily accessible to the citizenry.*

Reference List

Aguja, M. (n.d.). *Role of parliament in defence budgeting in the Philippines.* Retrieved from http://ipf-ssg-sea.net/userfiles/Explanatory%20Background%20Note%20Philippines.pdf

Aguja, M., & Born, H. (2017). *The role of parliament in police governance lessons learned from Asia and Europe.* Retrieved from DCAF: https://www.dcaf.ch/sites/default/files/publications/documents/The_Role_of_Parliament_in_Police_Governance.pdf

Aldis, A., & Drent, M. (2008). Common norms and good practices of civil-military relations in the EU. Retrieved from the Centre of European Security Studies: https://ciaotest.cc.columbia.edu/wps/cess/0018164/f_0018164_15578.pdf

Alford, R., & Friedland, R. (1992). Powers of theory. Cambridge: Cambridge University Press, DOI: https://doi.org/10.1017/CBO9780511598302

Allen, G., & Harding, M. (2021). *Police services Strength.* House of Commons Library, 17 September 2021. Retrieved from https://researchbriefings.files.parliament.uk/documents/SN00634/SN00634.pdf

Amnesty International. (2015). *Police Oversight Police and Human Rights Programme – Short paper series No. 2.* Retrieved from https://policehumanrightsresources.org/short-paper-series-no-2-police-oversight

Amnesty International. (2020). *Philippines: Duterte's coronavirus shoot-to-kill order is 'deeply alarming'.* Retrieved from Amnesty International UK: https://www.amnesty.org.uk/press-releases/philippines-dutertes-coronavirus-shoot-kill-order-deeply-alarming

Arnold, K. (2020, 29 April). *Army and police violence spurs racial tensions.* The Mail & Guardian. Retrieved from https://mg.co.za/article/2020-04-29-army-and-police-violence-spurs-racial-tensions/

Atienza, M.E. (2021). *The Philippines a year under lockdown.* Retrieved from https://verfassungsblog.de/the-philippines-a-year-under-lockdown/

Auditor-General South Africa. (2020). *Covid-19 Audit Report 2.* Retrieved from Auditor-General South Africa: https://www.agsa.co.za/Portals/0/Reports/Special%20Reports/Covid-19%20Special%20report/2020%202nd%20Covid-19%20Media%20Release%20FINALISEDFN.pdf

Bailes, A., & Holmqvist, C. (2007). *The increasing role of private military and security companies.* Retrieved from the European Parliament: https://www.europarl.europa.eu/cmsdata/175487/20080513ATT28807EN.pdf

Beliakova, P. (2021). Erosion of civilian control in democracies: A comprehensive framework for comparative analysis. *Comparative Political Studies, 54*(8), 1393–1423, DOI: https://doi.org/10.1177/0010414021989757

Bennett Institute for Public Policy. (2020). *The history of emergency legislation and the COVID-19 Crisis.* Retrieved from University of Cambridge: https://www.bennettinstitute.cam.ac.uk/blog/history-emergency-legislation-and-covid-19-crisis/

Booth, R. (2017, 23 May). *Soldiers on UK streets as threat raised to critical after Manchester bombing. The Guardian.* Retrieved from https://www.theguardian.com/uk-news/2017/may/23/salman-abedi-police-race-to-establish-if-manchester-suicide-bomber-acted-alone

Born, H. (2003). Parliamentary oversight of the security sector: Principles, mechanisms and practices (F. Philipp, A. Johnsson, & H. Born (eds.)). Retrieved from the DCAF: https://www.dcaf.ch/sites/default/files/publications/documents/ipu_hb_english_corrected.pdf

Brooks, R. (2020). Paradoxes of professionalism – Rethinking civil-military relations in the United States. *International Security, 44*(4), 7–44, DOI: https://doi.org/10.1162/ISEC_a_00374

Bruce, D. (2017). *Strengthening the independence of the Independent Police Investigative Directorate.* APCOF Policy Paper. February 2017. Retrieved from https://www.saferspaces.org.za/uploads/files/016-strengthening-the-independence-of-the-independent-police-investigative-directorate.pdf

Bryden, A., & Caparini, M. (eds.)(2006). Private actors and security governance. LIT and DCAF. Retrieved from: https://www.dcaf.ch/sites/default/files/publications/documents/bm_yb_2006.pdf

Bryman, A. (2008). Social research methods. Oxford: Oxford Universty Press, ISBN:9780199202959

Bucur-marcu, H. (2009). Essentials of defence institution building. Retrieved from the DCAF: https://www.files.ethz.ch/isn/129149/PAP-DIB_Bucur-IMS_FINAL.pdf

Burk, J. (2002). Theories of democratic civil-military relations. *Armed Forces & Society, 29*(1), 7–29. DOI: https://doi.org/10.1177/0095327X0202900102

Business World Online. (2014). *Security agencies a P49-B industry employing 670,000 – association.* Retrieved from: http://bworldonline.com/content.php?section=Economy&title=security-agencies-a-p40-b-industry-employing-670000----association&id=98468#:~:text=THE%20PRIVATE%20security%20services%20industry,to%20the%20positive%20economic%20conditions

Buzan, B. (1991). People, states and fear: An agenda for international security studies in the post-Cold War era. Birmingham : Harvester Wheatsheaf, ISBN: 9780745007205

Calland, R. (1997). All dressed up with nowhere to go: The rapid transformation of the South African Parliamentary Committee system. Cape Town: University of the Western Cape, ISBN: 1-86808-370-5

Capatides, C. (2020, April 2). *'Shoot them dead': Philippine President Rodrigo Duterte orders police and military to kill citizens who defy coronavirus lockdown.* Retrieved from CBS News: https://www.cbsnews.com/news/rodrigo-duterte-philippines-president-coronavirus-lockdown-shoot-people-dead/

Cervantes, F. M. (2020, March 24). *House okays special powers for PRRD to address Covid-19 crisis.* Retrieved from Philippine News Agency: https://www.pna.gov.ph/articles/1097565

Chitiyo, K. (2009). *The case for security sector reform in Zimbabwe* (p. 54). Retrieved from Royal United Services Institute: http://www.rusi.org/downloads/assets/Zimbabwe_SSR_Report.pdf

Cilliers, C. (2020, 30 March). *Watch: Police and SANDF force Soweto residents to do hard exercise as punishment. The Citizen.* Retrieved from https://citizen.co.za/news/south-africa/social-media/2262188/watch-police-and-sandf-force-soweto-residents-to-do-hard-exercise-as-punishment/

College of Policing. (2020). *Coronavirus Act 2020 (The Act) support public health.* Retrieved from College of Policing: https://www.college.police.uk/What-we-do/Support/Health-safety/Documents/Coronavirus-Act-2020-030420-public.pdf

Committee Affairs Department. (2020a). *Committee Daily Bulletin Vol. II No. 28*. Retrieved from Congress of the Philippines: https://www.congress.gov.ph/legisdocs/cdb/cdb18-v2i28-20200908 .pdf

Committee Affairs Department. (2020b). *Committee Daily Bulletin Vol. II No. 30*. Retrieved from Congress of the Philippines: https://www.congress.gov.ph/legisdocs/cdb/cdb18-v2i30 -20200910.pdf

Committee Affairs Department. (2020c). *Committee Daily Bulletin Vol. II No. 57*. Retrieved from https://www.congress.gov.ph/legisdocs/cdb/cdb18-v2i57-20201113.pdf

Committee Affairs Department. (2020d). *Committee Daily Bulletin Vol. I No. 82*. Retrieved from https://www.congress.gov.ph/legisdocs/cdb/cdb18-v1i82-20200310.pdf

Commons Select Committee Public Administration. (2020). *The Government's approach to legislation and the framework for parliamentary scrutiny*. Retrieved from UK Parliament: https:// publications.parliament.uk/pa/cm5801/cmselect/cmpubadm/377/37705.htm#_idText Anchor016

Congress of the Philippines. (2020). *Senate Resolution No. 479*. Retrieved from http://legacy .senate.gov.ph/lisdata/3319530042!.pdf

Cover, O., & Meran, S. (2013). *Watchdogs? The quality of legislative oversight of defence in 82 countries*. Retrieved from Transparency International: http://ti-defence.org/wp-content /uploads/2016/03/Watchdogs-low.pdf

CPBRD. (2020, May). *Special Issue: Covid-19 monitoring budgetary measures under the Bayanihan Act No. 2020-01*. Retrieved from Congressional Policy and Budget Research Department (CPBRD): https://cpbrd.congress.gov.ph/images/BB2020-01_Budgetary_Measures_For _Publication.pdf

Damgaard, E. (2000). Representation, delegation and parliamentary control. *ECPR Joint Sessions: Parliamentary Control of the Executive*. Copenhagen: Aarhus University.

Dandeker, C. (2013). Military contributions to non-traditional missions. In F. Vrey, A. Esterhuyse, & T. Mandrup (Eds.), *On Military Culture: Theory, practice and African armed forces* (pp. 35–48). Cape Town: UCT Press, ISBN: 978-1-177582-066-6

DCAF. (2006). *Parliamentary Committees on Defence and Security*. Geneva Centre for the Democratic Control of Armed Forces (DCAF). Retrieved from: https://www.files.ethz.ch /isn/15009/backgrounder_03_parliamentary_committees.pdf

DCAF. (2011) *Gender and Security Sector Reform: Examples from the Ground*. Geneva Centre for the Democratic Control of Armed Forces (DCAF). Retrieved from: https://dcaf.ch /gender-and-security-sector-reform-examples-ground

DCAF. (2015a) *Parliaments*. Geneva Centre for the Democratic Control of Armed Forces (DCAF). Retrieved from: https://dcaf.ch/sites/default/files/publications/documents/DCAF _BG_8_Parliaments.11.15.pdf

DCAF. (2015b). *Security Sector Governance*. Geneva Centre for the Democratic Control of Armed Forces (DCAF). Retrieved from: https://www.dcaf.ch/sites/default/files/publications /documents/DCAF_BG_1_SecuritySectorGovernance_0.pdf

DCAF. (2019). *Police Reform: Applying the principles of good security sector governance to policing*. SSR Backgrounder. DCAF – Geneva Centre for Security Sector Governance. Retrieved from: https://www.dcaf.ch/sites/default/files/publications/documents/DCAF_BG _16_Police%20Reform_0.pdf

DCAF. (2020). *DCAF webinar report: Parliament's role in linking good security sector governance to SDG16 amid COVID-19*. DCAF – Geneva Centre for Security Sector Governance. Retrieved from: https://dcaf.ch/sites/default/files/publications/documents/HLPF_Side_Event_Report _Parliament_SDG16_SSGR.pdf

De Vos, P. (2020). *What measures can the government legally take to deal with the coronavirus crisis?* Retrieved from Constitutionally Speaking: https://constitutionallyspeaking.co.za /what-measures-can-the-government-legally-take-to-deal-with-the-coronavirus-crisis/

Dearden, L. (2020). *Coronavirus: Woman fined 660 for refusing to tell police reasons for travel to have wrongful conviction quashed. Independent News.* Retrieved from https://www.independent.co.uk/news/uk/crime/coronavirus-fine-police-lockdown-travel-newcastle-marie-dinou-a9444186.html

Defence Subcommittee. (2020). *Women on the Armed Forces: From recruitment to civilian life.* Retrieved from UK Parliament: https://committees.parliament.uk/work/856/women-in-the-armed-forces-from-recruitment-to-civilian-life/

Dodd, V. (2020, 22 September). *Police dismiss idea of soldiers on UK streets to enforce Covid rules. The Guardian.* Retrieved from https://www.theguardian.com/world/2020/sep/22/police-dismiss-idea-of-soldiers-on-streets-to-enforce-covid-rules

Esterhuyse, A., & Heinecken, L. (2015). The Clausewitzian trinity: Reassessing the South African military's relationship with its polity and society. *Journal for Contemporary History, 1*(2), 71–95, ISSN 0285-2422

Evans, J. (2021). *Police holding internal probe on use of water cannons on Sassa applicants.* Retrieved from News24: https://www.news24.com/news24/southafrica/news/police-holding-internal-probe-on-use-of-water-cannons-on-sassa-applicants-20210120

Fabricius, P. (2020). *Brutal ISIS terror stalks northern Mozambique.* Retrieved from Daily Maverick: https://www.dailymaverick.co.za/article/2020-11-21-brutal-isis-terror-stalks-northern-mozambique/

Farge, E. (2020). *U.N. raises alarm about police brutality in lockdowns.* Retrieved from Reuters: https://www.reuters.com/article/us-health-coronavirus-un-rights-idUSKCN2291X9

February, J. (2006). More than a law-making production line? Parliament and its oversight role. In S. Buhlungu, J. Daniel, R. Southall & J. Lutchman (eds.), *State of the Nation 2005–2006* (pp. 123–142). Pretoria: Government Printers, ISBN 978-07969-2115-4

Ferreira, R. (2007). Civil-military relations and human security in South Africa. *Politeia, 26*(3), 229–251.

Ferreras, V. & Cachiles, G. (2020). *Retired soldier shot dead by police at checkpoint in Quezon City.* Retrieved from CNN Philippines: https://www.cnnphilippines.com/news/2020/4/22/Retired-soldier-shot-dead-by-police-.html

Fluri, P., & Lunn, S. (2010). *Oversight and guidance: The relevance of parliamentary oversight for the security sector* (P. Fluri & S. Lunn (eds.)). Retrieved from the DCAF: https://www.dcaf.ch/sites/default/files/publications/documents/Vademecum_v2.pdf

Fuior, T. (2011). Parliamentary powers in security sector governance (DCAF Parliamentary Programmes Series #1, Geneva: Geneva Centre for the Democratic Control of Armed Forces (DCAF), 2011).

Ghebali, V.-Y., & Lambert, A. (2004). *Democratic governance of the security sector beyond the OSCE area: Regional approaches in Africa and the Americas* (V.-Y. Ghebali & A. Lambert (eds.)). Retrieved from the DCAF: https://www.dcaf.ch/sites/default/files/publications/documents/Democratic_Governance_FINAL.pdf

Gillespie, T. (2021). *COVID-19: More than 42,000 fines issued by police for breacing coronavirus laws.* Retrieved from Sky News: https://news.sky.com/story/covid-19-more-than-42-000-fines-issued-by-police-for-breaching-coronavirus-laws-12201728

Gitari, C. (2019). *Situating security sector reforms in Kenya's discourse on inclusion and national dialogue process.* Retrieved from the International Center for Transitional Justice: https://www.ictj.org/sites/default/files/ICTJ_Briefing_KenyaInclusionDiscourse_Web.pdf

Gorbanova, M., & Wawro, L. (2011). *The Transparency of National Defence Budgets* (Anne-Christine Wegener (ed.)). Retrieved from Transparency International UK: http://ti-defence.org/wp-content/uploads/2016/03/2011-10_Defence_Budgets_Transparency.pdf

Gotinga, J. (2020). *Hontiveros calls for special audit of gov't spending on Covid-19 response.* Retrieved from Rappler: https://www.rappler.com/nation/hontiveros-calls-special-audit-government-spending-coronavirus-response

Gotinga, J. (2020a). *Senate ratifies Bayanihan 2 nill with P165.5 billion for pandemic response.* Retrieved from Rappler: a Government Gazette. (2020, 23 October). *The South African Government Gazette.* Retrieved from: https://www.gov.za/sites/default/files/gcis_document /202010/43834gen601_0.pdf

Gray, J., & Strasheim. J. (2016). Security sector reform, ethnic representation and perceptions of safety: Evidence from Kosovo. *Civil Wars, 18*(3), 338–358. DOI: https://doi.org/10.1080/1369 8249.2016.1215636

Grogan, J. (2020). *Parliament still does not have the power to scrutinise the Coronavirus Act 2020 properly.* Retrieved from The London School of Economics and Political Science (LSE): https://blogs.lse.ac.uk/covid19/2020/10/30/parliament-still-does-not-have-the -power-to-scrutinise-the-coronavirus-act-2020-properly/

Griffith, G. (2005). *Parliament and accountability: The role of parliamentary oversight committees* (Briefing Paper 12/05). Sydney: New South Wales Parliament.

Hague, R., & Harrop, M. (2007). *Comparative government and politics.* London: Palgrave Macmillan, ISBN: 9780230006379

Hänggi, H. (2003). Making sense of security sector governance. In H. Hanggi & T. Winkler (Eds.), *Challenges of security sector Governance* (pp. 3–23). Münster: LIT Verlag.

Hansard Society. (2021). *Coronavirus statutory instruments dashboard.* Retrieved from Hansard Society: https://www.hansardsociety.org.uk/publications/data/coronavirus-statutory -instruments-dashboard#powers-used-by-ministers

Hansard UK Parliament. (2021). *Covid-19 response: Defence Support Volume 687: debate on Tuesday 12 January 2021.* Retrieved from Hansard UK Parliament: https://hansard.parlia ment.uk/Commons/2021-01-12/debates/0A697A94-61F6-44E9-B58C-242C20AEB62C /Covid-19ResponseDefenceSupport

Head, T. (2020). *SANDF soldiers slammed for giving citizens 'humiliating punishmets'.* Retrieved from The South African: https://citizen.co.za/news/south-africa/social-media/2262188/watch -police-and-sandf-force-soweto-residents-to-do-hard-exercise-as-punishment/

Heinecken, L. (2009). A diverse dociety, a representative military? The complexity of manag- ing diversity in the South African armed forces. *Scientia Militaria – South African Journal of Military Studies, 37*(1), 25–49, ISSN: 1022-8136

Heywood, A. (1997). Politics. London: McMillan Press Limited. ISBN, 9781403989826.

Hollyer, J. R., Rosendorff, B. P., & Vreeland, J. R. (2011). Democracy and transparency. *Journal of Politics, 73*(4), 1191–1205. DOI: https://doi.org/10.1017/S0022381611000880

Home Affairs Committee. (2020). *Impact of Covid-19 on policing examined.* Retrieved from UK Parliament: https://committees.parliament.uk/work/184/home-office-preparedness-for -covid19-coronavirus/news/120195/impact-of-covid19-on-policing-examined/

Home Affairs Committee. (2020a). *Police conduct and complaints Inquiry.* Retrieved from UK Parliament: https://committees.parliament.uk/work/495/police-conduct-and-complaints /news/

Home Affairs Committee. (2020b). *The Macpherson Report: Twenty-one years on.* Retrieved from UK Parliament: https://committees.parliament.uk/work/347/the-macpherson-report -twentyone-years-on/

House of Commons. (2020). *Parliamentary scrutiny of the Government's handling of Covid-19.* Retrieved from UK Parliament: https://committees.parliament.uk/publications/3885/documents /38918/default/

House of Representatives Rules. (n.d.). *Rules of the House of Representatives 18th Congress, Part 3.* Retrieved from https://www.congress.gov.ph/download/docs/hrep.inquiries.rules.pdf

House Resolution 826. (2020). Retrieved from Philippine Congress: https://www.congress.gov.ph /legisdocs/basic_18/HR00826.pdf

House Resolution 832. (2020). Retrieved from Philippine Congress: https://www.congress.gov.ph /legisdocs/basic_18/HR00832.pdf

Hudson, K., & Henk, D. (2013). Strategising in an era of conceptual change: Security institutions and the delivery of security in the 21st century. In A. Esterhuyse, F. Vrey, & T. Mandrup (Eds.), *On military culture: Theory, practice and Afrian armed forces*. Cape Town: UCT Press, ISBN: 978-1-77582-066-6

Huntington, S. (1957). The Soldier and the state: The theory and politics of civil-military relations. Cambridge: Harvard University Press, ISBN: 9780674817364

Hyden, G., Court, J., & Mease, K. (2003). Civil Society and Governance in 16 Countries. In *Governance An International Journal Of Policy And Administration* (World Governance Survey Discussion Paper 4).

ICISS. (2001). *Report of International Commission on intervention and state sovereignty*. Retrieved from ICISS: https://www.idrc.ca/en/book/responsibility-protect-report-interna tional-commission-intervention-and-state-sovereignty

Inter-Parliamentary Union (IPU). (2013). *Enforcing the responsibility to protect: The role of parliaments in safguarding civilians' lives*. Retrieved from IPU: http://archive.ipu.org/PDF/128 /resolution-4-en.pdf

Izah, P. (2013). Legislative oversight and demcoracy in developing countries. *ECOWAS-P on Security Challenges and Political Instability in West Africa* (29–31 October 2013).

Janse van Rensburg, W. (2019). Twenty years of democracy: An analysis of parliamentary oversight of the military in South Africa since 1994. Stellenbosch: Stellenbosch University, ISSN: 2310-7855

Joint Committee on Human Rights. (2020). *Joint Committee on Human Rights Chair's briefing paper*. Retrieved from UK Parliament: https://publications.parliament.uk/pa/jt5801/jtselect /jtrights/correspondence/Chairs-briefing-paper-regarding-Health-Protection-Coronavirus -Restrictions-England-Regulation-2020.pdf

Kavanagh, S, Wardell, C, & Park, J (2020). *Time for change: A practical approach to rethinking police budgeting. GFOA Research Report*. Retrieved from: https://gfoaorg.cdn.prismic .io/gfoaorg/350fe9a8-57e6-4327-9e86-9fa97bd2a0d3_GFOA_TimeforChange_1.20.21 .pdf

Lalu, G. (2020). *Amid Covid-19 restrictions, COA looking to modernise auditing process*. Retrieved from Inquirer.Net: https://newsinfo.inquirer.net/1365738/amid-covid-19-restrictions -coa-looking-to-modernize-auditing-process

Lijphart, A. (1999). Patterns of Democracy. Yale: Yale University, ISBN: 978-0300078930

Lilly, A. (2020). *The UK parliament and coronavirus*. Retrieved from Institute for Government: https://www.instituteforgovernment.org.uk/explainers/uk-parliament-coronavirus

Lilly, A. & White, H. (2020a). *Parliament's role in the coronavirus crisis: Holding the Government to account*. Retrieved from Institute for Government: https://www.instituteforgovernment.org .uk/sites/default/files/publications/parliament-role-coronavirus-crisis-holding-government -account_0.pdf

Lima, R., Silva, P., & Rudzit, G. (2020). No power vacuum: National security neglect and the defence sector in Brazil. *Defence Studies*. 21(1), 1–23, DOI: https://doi.org/10.1080/1470243 6.2020.1848425

Mabuza, E. (2021). *SA mulls expunging criminal records of lockdown offencers, but not for multiple offenders*. Retrieved from TimesLive: https://www.timeslive.co.za/news/south-africa/2021 -01-18-sa-mulls-expunging-criminal-records-of-lockdown-offenders-but-not-for-multiple -offenders/

Mack, J., & Ryan, C. (2004). The perceived importance of the Annual Report. In C. Windson (Ed.), *Fourth One-Day Symposium on Accountability, Governance and Performance in Transition* (pp. 1–320). Southport: Griffith Business School.

Makinana, A. (2020). *Collins Khosa murder: Military Ombud finds that soldiers acted improperly*. Retrieved from Times Live: https://www.timeslive.co.za/politics/2020-08-19-collins-khosa -murder-military-ombud-finds-that-soldiers-acted-improperly/

Manila Standard. (2020). *Gov't eyes citizens groups to audit Covid19-related expenses*. Retrieved from Manilastandard.net: https://manilastandard.net/business/economy-trade/341882/gov-t -eyes-citizen-groups-to-audit-covid-19-related-expenses.html

Marais, S. & Azarrah, K. (2020). *Defence Minister Mapisa-Nqakula got it wrong on Collins Khosa inquiry, report is final – SANDF*. Retrieved from News24: https://www.news24.com/news24 /southafrica/news/defence-minister-mapisa-nqakula-got-it-wrong-on-collins-khosa -inquiry-report-is-final-sandf-20200605

Mills, L. (2017). *Parliamentary transparency and accountability*. Retrieved from: https://assets .publishing.service.gov.uk/media/59785450ed915d312c000005/081-Parliamentary-transpar ency-and-accountability.pdf

Möller-Loswick, A. (2017). *Is UN Goal 16 on peace being misused to justify securitization?* Retrieved from: https://theglobalobservatory.org/2017/10/is-un-goal-16-on-peace-being -misused-to-justify-securitization/

Montgomery, R and Griffiths, C. (2015). *The use of private security services for policing*. Retrieved from https://www.publicsafety.gc.ca/cnt/rsrcs/pblctns/archive-2015-r041/2015-r041-en.pdf

Namugwe, E. (2020). *COVID-19: Exceptional measures should not be cover for human rights abuses and violations*. Retrieved from United Nations: https://www.un.org.za/covid-19-exceptional -measures-should-not-be-cover-for-human-rights-abuses-and-violations-bachelet/

National Audit Office. (2020). *Defence capabilities – delivering what was promised*. Retrieved from National Audit Office UK: https://www.nao.org.uk/wp-content/uploads/2020/03/Defence -capabilities-delivering-what-was-promised-Summary.pdf

National Audit Office. (2020a). *The Equipment Plan 2019 to 2029*. Retrieved from National Audit Office UK: https://www.nao.org.uk/wp-content/uploads/2020/02/The-Equipment-Plan-2019 -to-2029-Summary.pdf

Obiyo, R. E. (2007). Legislative committees and deliberative democracy: The committee system of the South African Parliament with specific reference to the Standing Committee on Public Accounts (SCOPA). *Politeia*. 26(1), 60–79.

OHCHR. (2020). *OHCHR*. Retrieved from United Nations Human Rights Office of the High Commissioner: https://www.ohchr.org/Documents/Events/GoodPracticesCoronavirus /philippines-submission.docx

Olanday, D. & Rigby, J. (2020, 22 July). *Philippines turns to 'war on drugs' tactics to beat coronavirus, sparking human rights fears*. *The Telegraph*. Retrieved from https://www.telegraph.co.uk /global-health/science-and-disease/philippines-turns-war-drugs-tactics-beat-coronavirus -sparking/

Oliver, G. (2020). *Township lockdown: How South Africa's poor bear the cost of coronavirus*. Retrieved from The New Humanitarian: https://www.thenewhumanitarian.org/feature/2020/04/23 /South-Africa-coronavirus-jobs-poverty

Olson, D. M., Stapenhurst, R., Pelizzo, R., & von Trapp, L. (2008). Legislative oversight and budgeting: A world Perspective (L. von Trapp, R. Stapenhurst, D. M. Olson, & R. Pelizzo (eds.)). Washington: The World Bank, DOI: https://doi.org/10.1596/978-0-8213-7611-9

OpeningParliament.org. (2012). *Declaration on parliamentary openness*. Retrieved from: http:// www.openingparliament.org/

OSCE (2008). *Guidebook on Democratic Polcicing*. Retrived from https://www.osce.org/files/f /documents/5/3/23804.pdf

OSCE. (1994). *Code of conduct on politico-military aspects of security*. 91st Plenary Meeting of the Special Committee of the CSCS Forum for Security Co-Operation.

OSCE (2019). *The OSCE approach to security sector governance and reform (SSG/R) – Report by the Secretary General of the OSCE* (March 2019).

Parkinson, S. & Roe, C. (2020). *Parliamentary scrutiny in the time of Coronavirus*. Retrieved from Lexology: https://www.lexology.com/library/detail.aspx?g=62466d8f-c842-4b5e-835f-525 05140bd2f

Parliament RSA. (2020a). *Parliament of the Republic of South Africa*. Retrieved from Statement by the Presiding Officers of Parliament on the resumption of the business of Parliament, 16 April 2020: https://www.parliament.gov.za/press-releases/statement-presiding-officers-parliament -resumption-business-parliament-thursday-16-april-2020

Parliament RSA. (2020b). Announcements, Tablings and Committee Reports. 2020.

Parliament RSA. (2020c). *Changes in Parliament's programme due to Covid-19*. Retrieved from Parliament of the Republic of South Africa: https://www.parliament.gov.za/press-releases /change-parliaments-programme-due-covid-19

Parliament RSA. (2020d). *Constitutional obligations of Parliament during Covid-19 pandemic*. Retrieved from Parliament of the Republic of South Africa: https://www.parliament.gov.za /press-releases/constitutional-obligations-parliament-during-covid-19-pandemic

Parliament RSA. (2020e). *Deputy Speaker's response to DA Parliamentary Leader*. Retrieved from Parliament of the Republic of South Africa: https://www.parliament.gov.za/press-releases /deputy-speakers-response-da-parliamentary-leader

Parliament RSA. (2021). *Press Releases*. Retrieved from: https://www.parliament.gov.za /press-release

Pelizzo, R., Stapenhurst, R., & Olson, D. M. (2004). *Trends in parliamentary oversight*. Retrieved from World Bank: http://www.ssrn.com/abstract=1026338

Pelizzo, R., Stapenhurst, R., & Olson, D. (2006). *Parliamentary oversight for government accountability*. Retrieved from World Bank: https://www.agora-parl.org/sites/default/files/agora -documents/Parliamentary%20Oversight%20for%20Government%20Accountability.pdf

Philippine Congress. (2021). *The Private Security Industry Act*. Retrieved from: https://www .congress.gov.ph/legisdocs/basic_18/HB07037.pdf

Philippine House of Representatives. (2020). *Speaker Cayetano laudes 'unprecedented cooperation' between the executive and legislative to combat Covid-19*. Retrieved from Philippine House of Representatives: https://www.congress.gov.ph/press/details.php?pressid=11839 &key=covid

PMG. (2020a). *DoD 2020/21 Annual Performance Plans*. Retrieved from: https://pmg.org.za /committee-meeting/30141/

PMG. (2020b). *Police management of COVID-19 lockdown: SAPS briefing*. Retrieved from: https:// pmg.org.za/committee-meeting/30117/

PMG. (2020c). *Police misconduct in COVID-19 lockdown*. Retrieved from: https://pmg.org.za /committee-meeting/30164/

PMG. (2020d). *SANDF deployment & involvement in COVID-19 measures*. Retrieved from: https://pmg.org.za/committee-meeting/30107/

PMG. (2020e). *SAPS, IPID & CSPS Special Adjustments Budget*. Retrieved from: https://pmg.org .za/committee-meeting/30636/

PMG. (2021a). *DoD 2020/21 Quarter 2 & 3 performance & update on irregular expenditure and consequence management*. Retrieved from: https://pmg.org.za/committee-meeting/32449/

PMG. (2021b). *Joint Oversight Report to select Gauteng military bases & landline borders*. Retrieved from: https://pmg.org.za/committee-meeting/32379/

Provost, C. (2017). *The industry of inequality: why the world is obsessed with private security*. The Guardian. Retrieved from https://www.theguardian.com/inequality/2017/may/12 /industry-of-inequality-why-world-is-obsessed-with-private-security

PSIRA (2020). *Private Security Industry Regulatory Authority Annual Report 2019/20*. Retrieved from: https://www.psira.co.za/dmdocuments/Annual_Report_2020.pdf

Pulta, B. (2020). *PNP taps guards to help in quarantine duty*. Retrieved from Philippine News Agency: https://www.pna.gov.ph/articles/1097283

Punongbayan, J. (2020). *Analysis – How Duterte failed to the the Bayanhihan Law's objectives*. Retrieved from Rappler: https://www.rappler.com/voices/thought-leaders/analysis-how-duterte -failed-to-meet-bayanihan-law-objectives

Quinn, B. (2019, 22 February). Macpherson report: what was it and what impact did it have? *The Guardian*. Retrieved from https://www.theguardian.com/uk-news/2019/feb/22 /macpherson-report-what-was-it-and-what-impact-did-it-have

Republic of the Philippines. (2020). *Official Gazette*. Retrieved from: https://www.officialgazette .gov.ph/downloads/2020/03mar/20200316-PROC-929-RRD.pdf

Republic of the Philippines. (2020a). *Proclamation No. 1021: Extending the period of the State of Calaminity throughout the Philippines*. Retrieved from Presidential Communications Operations Office: https://pcoo.gov.ph/news_releases/proclamation-no-1021-extending-the -period-of-the-state-of-calamity-throughout-the-philippines-due-to-corona-virus-disease -2019-declared-under-proclamation-no-929-s-2020/

Republic of the Philippines. (2020b). *Philippines under State of Calamity due to Coronavirus.* Retrieved from Presidential Communications Operations Office: https://pcoo.gov.ph /news_releases/philippines-under-state-of-calamity-due-to-coronavirus/

Republic of the Philippines. (2020c). *Implement the law to fight Coronavirus, President Duterte tells local officials*. Retrieved from Presidential Communications Operations Office: https://pcoo .gov.ph/news_releases/implement-the-law-to-fight-coronavirus-president-duterte-tells-local -officials/

Repucci, S., & Slipowitz, A. (2020). *Democracy under lockdown*. Retrieved from Freedomhouse: https://freedomhouse.org/report/special-report/2020/democracy-under-lockdown

Reuters. (2020). *UK PM Johnson says army ready to step in of coronavirus escalates*. Retrieved from Reuters: https://www.reuters.com/article/us-health-coronavirus-britain-army/uk-pm -johnson-says-army-ready-to-step-in-if-coronavirus-escalates-idUSKBN20Q1C2

RLR Research and Analysis Inc. (2020). *Metro Manila Covid-19 opinion survey*. Retrieved from RLR Research and Analysis Inc: https://www.rlrresearch.com/metro-manila-covid -19-opinion-survey/

Roberts, A. (2007). Transparency in the security sector. In A. Florini (Ed.), *The right to know: Transparency for an open world* (pp. 309–336). New York: Columbia University Press, ISBN: 978-0-231-51207-7

Rozenberg, O. (2018) Why should parliaments continue to debate?: The intertwined virtues of parliamentary debates. *Redescriptions: Political Thought, Conceptual History and Femist Theory* 21(2), 148–66 DOI: http://dx.doi.org/10.7227/R.21.2.4

Russell, M. & James, L. (2020). *MPs are right. Parliament has been sidelined*. Retrieved from The Constitution Unit: https://constitution-unit.com/2020/09/28/mps-are-right-parliament -has-been-sidelined/

SABC News. (2020). *SANDF should not instill fear in people: Ramaphosa*. Retrieved from South African Broadcast Corporation (SABC): https://www.sabcnews.com/sabcnews/sandf -should-not-instil-fear-in-people-ramaphosa/

SABC News. (2021). *SANDF and SAHPRA brief Parliament on application to use Heberon for COVID-19 treatment*. Retrieved from South African Broadcast Corporation (SABC): https://www.sabcnews.com/sabcnews/sandf-and-sahpra-brief-parliament-on-application-to -use-heberon-for-covid-19-treatment/

Scheffer, D. (2008). Atrocity crimes framing the responsibility to protect in 40 Case Western Reserve. *Journal of International Law, 40*(1), 319–324 https://scholarlycommons.law.case.edu /jil/vol40/iss1/8

Schiff, R. (1995). Civil-military relations reconsidered: A theory of concordance. *Armed Forces & Society, 22*(1), 7–24, ISBN: 978-0-415-77340-9

Security Industry Authority (SIA). (2021a). *Covid-19 and the private security industry – Frequently asked questions*. Retrived from https://assets.publishing.service.gov.uk/government/uploads /system/uploads/attachment_data/file/1005296/sia-covid-19-faq.pdf

Security Industry Authority. (2020b). SIA approved contractors and license holders. Retrieved from SIA: https://www.gov.uk/government/statistical-data-sets/sia-approved-contractors

Southern African Legal Information Institute. (2020). *Khosa and Others v Minister of Defence and Military Defence and Military Veterans and Others (21512/2020) [2020] ZAGPPHC 147; 2020 (7) BCLR 816 (GP); [2020] 3 All SA 190 (GP); [2020] 8 BLLR 801 (GP); 2020 (5) SA 490 (GP); 2020 (2) SACR 461 (GP)* (15 May 2020). Retrieved from Southern African Legal Information Institute: http://www.saflii.org/za/cases/ZAGPPHC/2020/147.html

Sparrow, M. (2014). *Managing the boundary between public and private policing.* Harward Kennedy School. Retrieved from https://www.ojp.gov/pdffiles1/nij/247182.pdf

Stam, W. (2019). *International Day of UN Peacekeepers, a day of reflection.* Retrieved from Leiden University: https://www.thehagueuniversity.com/about-thuas/thuas-today/news/detail/2019/05/29/international-day-of-un-peacekeepers-a-day-of-reflection#:~:text=It was an improvised diplomatic,a soldier can do it'.

Tagarev, T. (2010a). *Building integrity and reducing corruption in defence: A compendium of best practices* (T. Tagarev (ed.)). Retrieved from the DCAF: https://www.dcaf.ch/sites/default/files/publications/documents/Compendium_Building_Integrity_and_Reducing_Corruption_in_Defence.pdf.

Tan, M. (2020). *Security Guards.* Retrieved from: https://opinion.inquirer.net/129537/security-guards#:~:text=Inquirer%20Board%20Chair%20and%20columnist,for%20the%20Philippine%20National%20Police

Toornstra, D. (2013). *Parliamentary oversight of the security sector.* Retrieved from European Parliament: https://www.dcaf.ch/sites/default/files/publications/documents/EP_Parliamentary_Oversight_Security_Sector_2013_BOH.pdf

Tumwebaze, V. et al. (2018). Corporate governance, internal audit function and accountability in statutory corporations. *Cogent Business and Management, 5*(1), 1–13. DOI: https://doi.org/10.1080/23311975.2018.1527054

UK Government. (2020). *Covid support force: The MOD's contribution to the coronavirus response.* Retrieved from Government of the UK: https://www.gov.uk/guidance/covid-support-force-the-mods-contribution-to-the-coronavirus-response

UK Parliament. (2021). *Covid-19 proceedings in the Commons Chamber.* Retrieved from UK Parliament: https://www.parliament.uk/about/how/covid-19-proceedings-in-the-house-of-commons/chamber-proceedings/

United Nations. (n.d). *What is the rule of law?* Retrieved from https://www.un.org/ruleoflaw/what-is-the-rule-of-law/

United Nations. (1945). *Charter of the United Nations.* Retrieved from UN: https://www.un.org/en/sections/un-charter/chapter-i/index.html

United Nations. (2005). *Responsibility to protect.* Retrieved from UN: https://www.un.org/en/genocideprevention/about-responsibility-to-protect.shtml

United Nations. (2008). *Sexual violence against women and children in conflict.* Retrieved from UN: http://archive.ipu.org/splz-e/unga08/s2.pdf

United Nations. (2015). *The Millennium Development Goals Report.* Retrieved from UN: DOI: https://doi.org/978-92-1-101320-7

United Nations. (2016). *The Sustainable Development Goals Report 2016.* Retrieved from UN: DOI: https://doi.org/10.1177/000331979004100307

United Nations. (2020). *'Toxic lockdown culture' of repressive coronavirus measures hits most vulnerable.* Retrieved from UN: https://news.un.org/en/story/2020/04/1062632?fbclid=IwAR3XlWVpwLY9c5ZWZRjSuo5s6IHKiHpG32W-brlSScOrXdKvowRFu0K1YZ0

United Nations Development Programme (UNDP). (1994). *Human Development Report: New Dimension of Human Security.* Retrieved from UNDP: http://hdr.undp.org/sites/default/files/reports/255/hdr_1994_en_complete_nostats.pdf

UNDP. (2002). *Human Development Report 2002: Deepening democracy in a fragmented world.* Retrieved from: http://hdr.undp.org/en/media/HDR_2002_EN_Complete.pdf

UNDP. (2017). *Parliaments' role in implementing the Sustainable Development Goals* (E. Lemieux, O. Pierre-Louveaux, & A. Mao (eds.)). Retrieved from UNDP: https://www.parlamericas.org /uploads/documents/ENG_Publication_SDGs.pdf

United Nations Office on Drugs and Crime (UNODC). (2011). *Handbook on police accountability, oversight and integrity*. Retrieved from https://www.unodc.org/pdf/criminal_justice/Hand book_on_police_Accountability_Oversight_and_Integrity.pdf

United Nations Office on Drugs and Crime (UNODC). (2014). *State regulation concering civilian private security services and their contribution to crime prevention and community safety*. Retrieved from the UNODC: https://www.unodc.org/documents/justice-and-prison-reform /Civilian_Private_Security_Services_Ebook.pdf

United Nations Office on Drugs and Crime (UNODC). (2020). *COVID-19 and Human Rights. We are all in this together*. April 2020. Retrieved from https://www.un.org/victimsofterrorism /sites/www.un.org.victimsofterrorism/files/un_-_human_rights_and_covid_april_2020.pdf

US Department of Defense. (2018) *Summary of the National Defence Strategy of the United States of America*. Retrieved from: https://dod.defense.gov/Portals/1/Documents/pubs/2018-National -Defense-Strategy-Summary.pdf

Vinci (2020). *Manned Security in 2020*. Retrieved from Vinci: https://www.vincifacilities.com /downloads/featured/manned-security-2020.pdf

Wallace, B. (2021). *Defence Secretary Oral Satement: Defence's COVID-19 support*. Retrieved from https://www.gov.uk/government/speeches/defence-secretary-oral-statement-defences -covid-19-support

White Paper on Policing (South Africa). (2016). Retrieved from http://www.policesecretariat.gov .za/downloads/bills/2016_White_Paper_on_Policing.pdf

Wurth, M. & Conde, C. (2020). *Philippine Children face abuse of violating Covid-19 curfew*. Retrieved from Human Rights Watch: https://www.hrw.org/news/2020/04/03/philippine -children-face-abuse-violating-covid-19-curfew

Yamamoto, H. (2007). *Tools for parliamentary oversight – A comparative study of 88 national parliaments*. Geneva: Inter-Parliamentary Union, ISBN: 978-92-9142-350-7

Yordanova, T. (2015, 6 June). *The transparency – security dilemma in national and international context (A comparative analysis of the UN and NATO's transparency/secrecy policies)*. Presented at the Fourth Global Conference on Transparency Research, Lugano, Switzerland.

www.ingramcontent.com/pod-product-compliance
Lightning Source LLC
Chambersburg PA
CBHW041431270326
41935CB00021B/1844